LUCY DANIELS

Animal Ark
Favourites

Illustrations by Jenny Gregory

*Hodder
Children's
Books*

a division of Hodder Headline plc

Special thanks to Helen Magee, Jenny Oldfield and Sue Welford.
Thanks also to C. J. Hall, B.Vet.Med., M.R.C.V.S., for reviewing
the veterinary information contained in this book.

First published in Great Britain in 1998
by Hodder Children's Books

A Catalogue record for this book is available from the British Library

ISBN 0 340 69958 2

Typeset by Avon Dataset Ltd, Bidford-on-Avon, Warks

Printed and bound in Great Britain by
Clays Ltd, St Ives plc

Hodder Children's Books
a division of Hodder Headline plc
338 Euston Road
London NW1 3BH

Contents

Sheepdog on show

'Come in! Away to me!' Dora Janeki gave the shrill shepherd's command.

Her dog, Whistler, streaked around the back of a bunch of sheep and began herding them down the hill.

'He's fast,' James Hunter muttered. He watched with narrowed eyes.

'Fast isn't everything,' Mandy Hope countered. 'Anyway, Tess is fast too.'

They sat on the stone wall at Syke Farm, judging every detail of the grey sheepdog's performance. Dora's brother, Ken Hudson, stood nearby with his own dog, Tess.

Dora whistled. 'Away to me!' she shouted again.

Whistler herded the sheep to the right, steering them clear of a steep drop.

'Lie down!' Dora cried.

The dog stopped and crouched. The sheep jostled clumsily.

'He does exactly as he's told,' James noted. He knew Whistler was an experienced working dog, well trained and reliable.

'So does Tess.' Mandy jumped down from the wall to crouch beside her favourite.

James frowned. 'But Whistler's got more experience,' he pointed out. 'He's won two championship ribbons already!'

'So?'

Tess wagged her bushy tail as Mandy put an arm around her. She gazed at Mandy with trusting, dark brown eyes, nudging her hand with her soft, black nose.

'You're a brilliant sheepdog, every bit as good as Whistler. And I'm sure you can beat him,' she whispered.

Tess and Whistler were rivals. Dora had trained Whistler to follow her every command. Her brother, Ken, who lived with Dora at Syke Farm, had adopted Tess after Mandy and James had rescued her as a young dog. She'd grown sleek and fit, with her black ears and white muzzle, her white chest and black back, and her lovely white-tipped tail.

'Come by!' Dora cried.

Whistler surged forward once more, circling the sheep to keep them in a tight bunch. He brought them close to where Dora stood.

'That'll do!' She gave one last command.

The dog came and sat at her side, tongue lolling, sides heaving, while the sheep relaxed and began to nibble the short grass.

Dora turned to her audience, her head high. 'What did you think of that?'

'Brilliant!' James smiled and nodded.

'He's very good,' Mandy said more guardedly, one arm still around Tess's neck.

'Not bad,' Ken sniffed. No way would he let his sister see that he was impressed. Instead, he pulled his flat cap down over his wrinkled forehead and got ready to put Tess through her paces.

Dora tutted. 'Admit it, your dog's no match for mine.'

'I'll admit no such thing,' Ken grunted back. He whistled Tess to him.

Tess left Mandy and bounded to Ken's side, eager to begin work. She sat obediently to wait for the next command.

'Two red ribbons!' Dora reminded them, as she set

off with Whistler across the farmyard towards the barn. 'And a third to join them on my mantelpiece, come this Sunday!'

Mandy narrowed her eyes and pretended not to hear. She watched Tess begin to herd the sheep back up the hillside. *Don't count your chickens*! she thought silently. Tess was young, strong and clever. Very clever in fact. Ken had only to whistle a command for her to guide the sheep wherever he wanted them: behind a clump of trees, between boulders, or up into the heather.

'That'll do!' he called, and brought Tess sprinting down the hill back towards the farm. The small, bow-legged farmer stooped to pat his dog.

Mandy and James ran to join them. 'That was excellent!' Mandy gasped. 'She didn't put a foot wrong!'

Ken grunted. 'She's just about ready,' he agreed.

Ready for the Welford Sheepdog Trials this coming Sunday. Keen and fit, Tess had been beautifully trained by the wizened ex-pigman. But was she good enough to beat Whistler and all the other Border collies on show at the weekend?

As Mandy knelt to make a fuss of Tess, stroking her and tickling her behind her ears, she heard the farmer express his one doubt about the dog.

'Don't tell Dora I said this,' he murmured, glancing

over his shoulder towards the farm. 'But the trouble with Tess is, she sometimes gets put off the job in hand.'

'What do you mean?' James asked.

'It's because she's not a farm dog born and bred,' Ken explained. 'She might lose concentration if I'm not careful, and I reckon I'll have my work cut out on Sunday. There'll be a big crowd at the show; lots of distractions.'

'No problem!' Mandy insisted. 'Tess will behave herself, won't you, girl?'

Tess nudged her hand to be stroked again.

'You won't be put off. You'll be perfect!' Mandy pictured the red rosette pinned to Tess's collar at the end of a hard-fought contest. 'Tess the champion!' she sighed, crossing her fingers and staring up the hillside as if she could see the future there. 'Tess the number one sheepdog in the whole of Welford!'

The following Saturday, at home at Animal Ark, Adam Hope put down the phone. 'Well, fancy that!' He shook his head and began to hum.

Mandy could tell he was pleased. She was in the kitchen with her gran, busily making cakes and scones for the coffee stall at the next day's trials. Her mum was out on a call at the Spillers' smallholding on the moor.

Gran Hope glanced up from scooping cake mixture into a tin, her face flushed from the oven. 'Fancy what, dear?'

'Don't ask him,' Mandy warned. 'He's doing it on purpose.' She knew her dad was hugging his secret to himself to tease them.

'*Me*!' he chirped. 'They asked *me*!'

'Asked you what?' A head appeared around the door: a head with a wide-brimmed, peacock-blue hat on it. 'Does it have anything to do with the judging of the sheepdog trials tomorrow, by any chance?' The voice matched the hat – loud and demanding attention.

Mandy heard her gran swallow a groan.

Adam Hope jumped back, then recovered. 'Hello there, Mrs Ponsonby!'

The bossy old lady came in with her two dogs. 'It does, doesn't it?' she cooed. 'I know; don't tell me. The organisers of the contest have asked you to present the prizes!'

Mandy stared. Out of the corner of her eye, she noticed her gran turn her back and splash the cake-mix bowl into a sink full of soapy water. Pandora, Mrs Ponsonby's Pekinese, smelt food and jumped up at the table. Toby, her good-natured mongrel, snuffled around the floor for crumbs.

'How did you know that?' Adam Hope asked, his jaw hanging.

Mrs Ponsonby laughed richly and tapped the side of her nose. 'Let's just say a little birdie told me!'

'As a matter of fact, you're right,' Mandy's dad admitted. 'And I accepted.'

'I said you would!' A knowing wink followed. 'I told them, who better than the local vet to present the prizes? Of course, that was after their first choice had let them down at the last minute. But I was sure you wouldn't mind stepping into the breach, Adam!'

'Er-hum!' Dorothy Hope stopped busybody Amelia Ponsonby in mid-flow.

Mandy hid a grin. Trust Mrs Ponsonby to know everything, to be everywhere, to organise the whole world without being asked.

Except, of course, her dogs. 'Down, Toby! Down, Pandora!' the old lady cried, but the two unruly creatures snuffled at Gran's legs.

'What can we do for you?' Gran asked, redder in the face than ever.

Mrs Ponsonby opened her large shiny handbag and produced a pen and paper. 'I'm making a list of the cakes for tomorrow's stall,' she announced. 'Size, flavour and quantity.' She stood with pen poised. 'Perhaps you would allow me to add your contribution, Dorothy?'

And, much as Mandy's gran protested that it was hardly necessary, Mrs Ponsonby insisted.

'For it would be a disaster if we were to end up with fifty chocolate cakes and no rich fruit!' she proclaimed. 'And my information will be handy as a price list. You see, it pays to be well prepared. Prices, napkins, plates, table linen: I've thought of everything.' She wrote with a heavy hand. 'Is that carrot cake I can smell? Such a good standby cake. So healthy!'

'Three carrot cakes,' Dorothy Hope said through gritted teeth. 'Three rich fruit, and *no* chocolate!'

Mandy saw her gran step accidentally on Pandora's fluffy foot. The dog squeaked and dashed to the door. She grinned at her dad and let the two old ladies battle politely on.

'My money's on Dora Janeki's dog again.' Ernie Bell had come up to The Beacon on the morning of the trials. He followed a steady stream of cars out of the village on to the high pastures behind Lydia Fawcett's farm at High Cross, where the annual sheepdog show was held.

'I'm not so sure,' Walter Pickard replied. 'There are plenty of other good dogs competing this year. I fancy Gwen, Jack Spiller's little bitch. She's a real stayer.'

Mandy stood with James in the queue behind the two old men. It seemed everyone had an opinion.

'What about young Brandon Gill's chances?' Lydia herself had strolled over from her goat farm, dressed as ever in a thick woollen jacket and wellingtons, though the day had dawned bright and clear. 'This is the first year he's entered the competition, but from what I hear he's working his father's dog, Brandy, the one Ken Hudson used to show up here in the days when he worked for the Gills.'

'Brandy's a useful dog,' Ernie agreed.

'But Ken must fancy himself with his new one, what's-its-name?' Walter pointed out.

'Tess!' Mandy jumped in with the required information as the queue moved slowly through the entrance gate. 'We've seen her. You wouldn't believe how good she is!'

'You're biased,' Walter grunted. 'Anyhow, I expect Ken will be dead set on beating his sister.'

Ernie nodded but still stuck with his first opinion. 'Dora's dog is the one with the experience. Five pounds on Whistler,' he repeated. 'If I was a betting man, that's where I'd put my money!'

'Tess can do it!' Mandy repeated the magic phrase to herself. She'd left James talking to Brandon Gill and made her way towards the coffee stall, looking out in the crowd for a sight of Ken Hudson. Contestants mingled with onlookers, keeping a wary eye on the three judges clustered together around a plain trestle table. Beyond them was a wide open stretch of hillside

marked out with bales of straw and coloured flags.
And to the far side of the arena stood a row of Land-
rovers and trailers containing the sheep that were soon
to be let loose for the start of the trials.

Mandy took a deep breath. No sign so far of Ken
and Tess. Perhaps he wanted to keep his dog well out
of the way until their turn came. He would want her
to stay calm. There was this worry about her being
put off by crowds . . . Yes, she was sure Ken would
show up at the last minute, keeping Tess's mind fixed
on the job in hand. Slowly Mandy edged her way
through the crush.

'That's one pound and thirty pence!' Mrs
Ponsonby's voice rang out above the buzz of the
people gathered around the coffee stall. 'Ah, Mandy
dear, there you are!'

Mandy sank back behind a tall figure, but in vain.

'Just in time to take coffee and cake to the judges
before the competition begins!'

A plump hand seized her by the arm and dragged
her inside the refreshment marquee. Toby and
Pandora tangled themselves between her legs, glad
to see her too. Behind the counter Mandy's gran was
quietly serving the hot drinks and slicing cakes while
Mrs Ponsonby ruled the roost in her buttercup yellow
hat and frilly white blouse. Mandy saw her mum and
dad talking in a corner with James's parents.

'Down, Pandora; there's a darling!' The owner of
Bleakfell Hall ignored the fact that Pandora had just
snaffled a lemon scone off someone's paper plate.
She loaded a tray and handed it to Mandy. Then she
turned her about and ordered her out to the judges'
table. 'Come back in the interval,' she ordered. 'I may
need you again!'

Mandy left the tent with the groaning tray. 'Down,
Toby!' she muttered. The mongrel had almost
knocked her off balance.

Seeing her frowning face, her mum came to the
rescue. She grabbed Toby's collar before he could
jump up again and gave Mandy a sympathetic smile.
'Never mind,' she whispered. 'At least you'll have a
good view if you stay close to the judges' table.'

And this proved to be true. As Mandy arrived with
the refreshments at the edge of the arena, the first
sheep had been let loose, and Jack Spiller's Gwen had
begun work on the hill. The three judges had eyes
only for the skilful dog.

'Come by, Gwen!' Mr Spiller steered her off to the
left. One judge nodded and ticked a box on his scoring
sheet.

'Now, come in!' The smallholder ordered his dog
to herd the closely-bunched sheep between two flag-
markers. When one of the sheep broke away, a second
judge shook his head.

'That's torn it,' a member of the audience muttered. Gwen and Jack Spiller had been put out of the running by one small mistake.

Then it was Brandon Gill's turn with Brandy. Mandy and James's schoolfriend looked nervous as he entered the arena. But he managed to forget the onlookers and get on with the task. He sent Brandy out on a fetch, calling and whistling at exactly the right moment, as the dog ran and crouched, shifting the sheep from right to left, bundling them through the markers and finally into the pen made from straw bales. 'Right, that'll do!' Brandon cried, and the lithe black and white dog came running swiftly to his call.

'Not bad,' another voice in the crowd said, while the judges ticked boxes and looked impressed.

Mandy had stayed quietly beside the judges' table, enjoying her ring-side view. She could see the names written in order on the nearest man's score sheet. Next came two farmers from the neighbouring dale with dogs she didn't know. Then Dora Janeki, with Whistler.

'Last year's winner.' One judge murmured a reminder to his colleagues. They seemed to sit up and pay particular attention as the strange-looking, grey-haired dog appeared in the arena.

Mandy studied Whistler hard. What was it about him that set him apart from the other dogs? True, he was long-legged and swift. True, he had a determined, arrow-straight way of shooting off up the hill in pursuit of the sheep. He kept low, never taking his eye off the flock, never for a moment letting one slip away.

And Dora, small and skinny as she was, let them all know who was boss, dog and sheep alike. She whistled and cried out, watching them with an expert eye, changing her call, working the sheep through the markers in record time.

Tick, tick, tick went the judges' biros on the score sheets. Never a foot wrong.

'Wonderful,' came the voices in the crowd. 'Sheer brilliance. Poetry in motion.'

Mandy heard, and her heart sank. Dora's poker-straight face didn't give anything away as she walked Whistler out of the arena, but her head was high, her shoulders back. She knew that her dog had given a near perfect performance. Would Ken and Tess ever be able to match that?

'One more to go before half-time.' One of the judges looked at his watch, then glanced at the next names on the list. 'Ken Hudson, with a new dog I've never heard of before.'

Mandy was looking round anxiously for her first view of Tess when a voice carried above the hush of the expectant crowd.

'Clear the way!' it called. 'Make room there!'

The crowd parted for Mrs Ponsonby just as Ken and Tess finally put in their appearance at the far side of the arena. Unaware of the interruption, Ken began work as the old woman's wide-brimmed hat bobbed towards the judges.

'Wait.' The nearest judge raised his arm in vain to delay Ken, who seemed put off his stride. All heads turned to stare at Mrs Ponsonby, tray in hands, followed by her two spoiled pets.

'More coffee for the judges!' Mrs Ponsonby called, while Pandora and Toby rioted between people's legs.

Mandy jumped to her feet and whispered, 'Not now!'

Tess had noticed the disturbance and cocked her head to one side. Then she heard Ken whistle another command. She drove the sheep forward into the centre of the arena, trying hard to concentrate.

'Later!' Mandy pleaded.

But Mrs Ponsonby wasn't going to wait for anyone. She ploughed ahead to plant the tray of refreshments on the judges' table.

'Come in, Tess!' Out on the field, Ken struggled to keep control. The dog herded the sheep into a tight knot.

The judges had to peer past Mrs Ponsonby's ample figure to see what was happening in the arena. Toby got his front paws on to the table to snatch at a tempting cake.

Mandy groaned. If Ken and Tess could keep going through all this it would be a miracle.

'Pandora, come back!' Mrs Ponsonby's voice rose again. Her plump hands flew to her mouth as a streak of light fawn fur bounded out into the trials arena. Pandora had spotted Tess's game with the sheep. She wanted to join in.

The crowd gasped at the sight of the podgy Pekinese. Ken was about to steer the sheep between two vital markers. If Pandora distracted Tess now, all would be lost.

It was time for rapid action. As Mrs Ponsonby cried and waved her arms after her naughty dog, Mandy did the only thing possible to save the day for Ken and Tess. She rugby-tackled Mrs Ponsonby's pesky pet.

She went full length, arms outstretched. Pandora swerved, but too late. Mandy landed on her stomach with a mouthful of grass. But she had the dog clutched tight in her arms.

'More of a desperate dive and a wrestle than a rugby tackle,' her dad said later, as he was about to present the prizes.

Mandy grinned ruefully. She stood at his side, holding the three rosettes in readiness.

'Not that I'm criticising,' Adam Hope told her. 'It certainly did the trick.' He laughed and shook his

head. 'But who'd have thought it of Pandora!'

Mandy recalled how she'd kept firm hold of Pandora and bribed Mrs Ponsonby's two dogs to stay put by feeding them titbits, while Ken put Tess through her paces. Tess had been brilliant. She'd ignored the rude disturbance and worked on; darting here and there, crouching and worrying the sheep into the pen.

Tick-tick, *tick-tick*. The judges' biros had scored Tess's sheet.

'Good girl, that'll do!' Ken had called at last, his voice pleased. Tess had trotted back to him, tail up, ears pricked. They both knew they had done a fine job.

And now it was over. Others had had their turn, and the competition had moved on. The day had passed in ever more complicated tasks for the shepherds and their dogs. In the end, it was clear that the red ribbon was between the two outstanding performers: Whistler and Tess.

'. . . Third prize goes to Brandon Gill with his dog, Brandy!' the chief judge announced. Shy Brandon glowed with pleased embarrassment as he walked up to take his rosette from Mr Hope.

Mandy held her breath. The clapping died away. The judge was about to announce the runner-up. Would it be Tess or Whistler? She could see Ken and Dora hovering at the edge of the arena, their dogs sitting obediently to heel.

The judge cleared his throat. 'Second prize this year to . . . Whistler and Dora Janeki of Syke Farm!'

Dora and Ken shook hands. Last year's winner came forward amidst loud applause to take the runner's-up ribbon.

'And our champion team for this year is . . . newcomer Tess, with Ken Hudson!'

There was a cheer. For a few seconds Mandy closed her eyes. Then her dad pushed her forward, urging her to fix the red rosette to Tess's collar. The dog gazed up with enormous brown eyes, her tail wagging to and fro. Ken shook hands with the judges, with her dad, and with Mandy herself.

'Thanks,' he murmured with a special look and a nod. Ken wasn't a man of many words; still he realised that Mandy's quick thinking had saved the day.

'What he means to say is, his dog won first prize thanks to you,' Dora leaned across to explain.

But Mandy smiled and shook her head. She wouldn't take the credit. 'I always knew Tess could do it.'

The red ribbon fluttered in the breeze against the dog's shiny black and white coat.

'From the moment James and I rescued her on the snowy moor, I knew in my heart Tess was a champion!'

*Read more about Tess's adventures in **Sheepdog in the Snow**.*

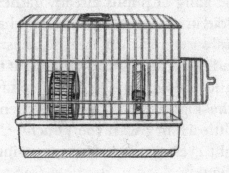

Hamster on the run

'Class dismissed!' The bell had gone and Miss Temple, the biology teacher, signalled the start of lunchbreak at Walton Moor School.

'Thank heavens! I'm starving,' Vicki Simpson sighed, gathering her books. 'Come on, Becky, let's go and grab a table.'

'OK.' Becky Severn joined the scramble for the door. 'You coming, Mandy?'

But Mandy didn't hear. She was too busy trying to attract Miss Temple's attention. 'Miss Temple! Miss!' Her voice rose above the scraping of chairs and shuffling of feet.

'What is it, Mandy?' The teacher peered over the

heads of the gang of pupils already gathered at the lab door. 'Hold it, everyone. Let me hear what Mandy's trying to say.'

Mandy had done what she always did at the end of a lesson in the biology lab: she'd gone to say goodbye to Henry the Eighth, the school's golden hamster; fat, furry little Henry with the pouchy cheeks and button bright eyes; greedy Henry, peering cheekily out of his cage.

Except that today he wasn't.

Mandy had looked in every corner of the cage, among the heap of paper in his sleeping compartment, inside the exercise wheel where he would endlessly tread. But there had been no hamster there.

'Henry's vanished!' she cried across the room. 'He's not in his cage. He's escaped again!'

'All right now, everyone, calm down!' Miss Temple acted quickly. She asked the class to move carefully back to their places, and made sure that the lab doors were shut. 'Henry's done this before and he never goes far. I want you to check your bags before you leave. I wouldn't put it past him to have snuck inside for a taste of someone's packed lunch!'

'How did he get out?' Vicki asked.

Becky checked her bag, then shrugged. 'You know what he's like. Give him a sniff of a sandwich and he can escape from anywhere!'

It wasn't the first time Henry had gone on the run. The greedy little hamster might be fat, but he was nippy and clever. Mandy reckoned he would have seized his chance to make a run for it if someone had left the cage door even slightly open, by mistake. She searched her bag, then under the work benches, listening for the scuttle of his sharp little claws.

'Don't worry class, we'll soon find him.' Miss Temple had joined the search. Her wavy brown hair swung across her face as she poked among the piles of textbooks beside Henry's cage.

'Miss, I'm hungry!' a voice complained from beside the door. It belonged to Vicki's twin brother, Justin.

'So am I!'

'Me too!'

'Miss, can we go and have our lunch?'

Several others began to protest about being kept from their lunch.

'OK, this is what we'll do,' the teacher replied. 'In a moment, those people who want to leave will be free to do so, quietly and carefully.'

'But what about Henry?' Becky murmured.

'We can't just forget about him!' Vicki agreed.

Mandy said nothing. She just kept on searching.

Miss Temple continued. 'And those who want to carry on looking for Henry can stay behind. But before any of you decide, let me say that it is important to find Henry before the end of the school day. If he stays missing overnight, then we'll have much less chance of tracking him down. Today's Friday, of course, and the weekend is a long time for him to be on the run.'

Mandy frowned and took a good look behind the rows of geranium pots on the windowsill.

'So, what I'm going to do to encourage you all to do your very best to track him down is to offer a reward!'

'*Reward?*' Suddenly those who'd wanted to leave were interested again.

Miss Temple went to stand with them, ready to let them out. 'Whoever finds Henry, and returns him safely, will be let off this week's biology homework.'

'No biology homework! . . . That's worth missing lunch for! . . . Count me in!' Eager voices began to organise small search parties to recapture the hamster.

'Think where a hamster would head in a big building like this. Try to outwit him,' the teacher advised.

'Becky, you can be my partner!' Vicki seized her friend's arm and dragged her into the corridor as the rush to find Henry began. 'Come on, let's get a move on.'

Vicki and Becky disappeared after the other eager searchers.

'What about you, Mandy?' Miss Temple asked. 'Who will you team up with?'

Mandy had stayed behind, peering into every corner of the room until she was sure that Henry's bid for freedom had taken him beyond the lab. 'I'll ask James,' she decided. 'Once I tell him what's going on, he'll want to help.'

'Well, good luck.' Miss Temple was on her way out too. 'I know you two will use your heads instead of dashing into things.'

Mandy pushed her blonde hair behind her ears and slung her bag over her shoulder. James could always come up with a plan. But first she had to find her friend and explain.

'. . . Where would he run to?' That was the big question. Mandy put it to James once she'd found him standing by his locker outside the cloakroom.

James thought long and hard. Justin Simpson and his mates dashed by, flinging open classroom doors and crawling under desks in a mad search for Henry.

'. . . Not in here! . . . No sign of the stupid thing!' Doors swung and banged, and trainers squeaked on down the corridor.

'Concentrate on what Henry would be likely to do once he got out of the cage.' James took things much more slowly. He went on absentmindedly opening his locker to take out his lunch-box.

The plastic container caught Mandy's eye. 'Food!' she said suddenly. 'He'd be looking for something to eat!' That was why Miss Temple had made them search their bags.

James nodded. 'And where would he look?' He reached for his sandwiches. 'Where do people keep their food?'

Mandy turned her head to look along the row of metal lockers. A dozen kids were doing exactly what James had just done: unlocking the doors and reaching for their sandwiches and crisps. Her eyes widened. She turned back to James.

'Here!' they said together.

'Aagh!' A small girl along the row stepped back and screamed. She dropped her lunch on the floor. A red apple rolled under the radiator.

'Henry!' Mandy cried.

'It's a rat! There's a rat in my locker!' the girl cried.

'It's not a rat, it's a hamster! Close the door!' James yelled at her, as he and Mandy began to sprint down the row. 'Keep him inside! Don't let him escape!'

But the girl was too shocked to move. As her apple rolled out of sight, Mandy and James heard a scrabbling sound against the metal floor of the locker, and saw a flash of golden brown and white fur as a small animal leaped to the floor.

'It is, it's Henry!' Mandy dropped on to all fours and crawled between legs to reach him. There he was, pursuing the apple, his short legs scurrying over the grey floor tiles, his fat body squeezing under the radiator after it.

As he sank his sharp front teeth into the sweet fruit, she made a lunge.

Henry sensed Mandy hurtling towards him. His long whiskers twitched, his round ears went back and he sighed. He would have to give up the apple. In a flash, as Mandy stretched out her cupped hands, he reared up, turned and scuttled away.

'Nearly!' James sighed.

Mandy stood up and brushed herself down. Her knees and elbows hurt from her crash landing.

Word had got out that Henry had been spotted. Feet thundered back up the corridor, voices shouted and locker doors creaked and slammed.

'If he's got any sense, he'll be miles away from here by now,' Vicki Simpson said in a high, know-it-all way. She stared suspiciously from behind a row of lockers at Mandy and James as if they knew more than they were saying.

'Let's try the Home Economics room!' her partner, Becky Severn, whispered, tugging at Vicki's sleeve.

'Shh! Good idea!' Vicki's broad, freckled face

disappeared. The two girls crept off down the corridor.

'More food!' Mandy had overheard Becky's new plan. And now she came to think of it, there was a delicious smell of baking coming from the Home Economics room – warm, sweet and fresh. Any self-respecting hamster in need of a bite to eat would follow up that smell straight away.

'Let's try!' James agreed.

So they tiptoed after Vicki and Becky, away from the chaos by the lockers into the peace and quiet of the cooker-lined room, where surfaces gleamed and posters listing food values covered the walls. Set out on racks on a central table were rows of freshly-baked sponge cakes.

'This was our idea!' Vicki turned on Mandy and James as soon as they entered the room. 'You can't come in!'

'Shh!' Mandy warned. If Henry had scuttled in here, following his sharp pink nose, they all needed to keep quiet and not scare him off again.

James ignored Vicki and began to search for the runaway.

'We can't stop them,' Becky hissed at Vicki. 'Everyone's allowed to look!'

Scowling, Vicki turned her back. 'If you get let off biology homework, Mandy Hope, I'll say it's not fair!'

Just because Mandy loved animals, she was Miss Temple's favourite; everyone knew that.

'Let's try the stock cupboard,' James whispered to Mandy. 'It might be a bit exposed for Henry out here. He likes to stay hidden if he can.'

So they left Vicki and Becky checking for telltale crumbs and bite-marks in the tempting cakes and went to look in the small shelf-lined cupboard. There were packets of flour, cartons of eggs, jars of honey, jam . . . and Henry!

Henry was tucking into a feast of strawberry jam, his front paws red and sticky, his whiskers dripping with juice. He looked up guiltily as James and Mandy caught him in the act. His short-sighted eyes blinked,

his nose twitched again . . . and he was off!

Down from the shelf, leaving a trail of jammy footprints, he landed with a heavy thump, his fat, golden body as round as a ball. But he was still speedy.

'Watch out!' James warned. Henry had nipped between his legs, and he was out in the main room, heading for the door and freedom.

'Henry, come back!' Mandy scooted after him, leaving Vicki and Becky standing. Henry was making for the Art Room nearby, in through the open door and up on a table where paintings had been left to dry.

'Oh no!' James groaned as Henry waddled across the wet paint.

Mandy saw what he was up to and covered her eyes. Peeping between her fingers, she saw the hamster stop and sit up on his haunches. He wrinkled his nose and looked this way and that. *What, no food?*

No; just a trail of bright paw-prints across the pad of clean white paper as he went on his way. Red, yellow, blue and green.

'Henry's an artist!' Mandy grinned in spite of everything.

He sat down again, front paws tucked under his chin, studying the pattern he'd made. Then the door behind them was blocked with kids all claiming that they'd found the hamster and got him trapped.

Miss Temple came hurrying over and tried to clear the way. Henry heard it all with a weary sigh. The game was up; time to head for home.

'Look, he seems to want us to get close!' Mandy spotted the change in Henry, who sat quietly watching them, ignoring the crush that was going on in the doorway.

'You do it!' James urged. 'Go on, Mandy, he knows you best!' He realised that the tame hamster would trust her.

'OK, Henry!' She nodded and approached firmly, expecting him at any second to change his mind and scuttle off again. He sat, dangling his paint-covered front paws, cocking his ears, waiting.

'There's a good boy.' Mandy was very close now. She leaned forward with cupped hands.

'Miss, that's not fair!' Suddenly Vicki Simpson shouted and broke through the crowd of onlookers. She rushed into the Art Room, pointing at Mandy and James. '*They* didn't find Henry; *we* did! He was in the Home Economics room. We thought of it first!'

Mandy groaned. Vicki's high-pitched voice had upset the hamster. In a flash Henry was gone again; down from the table, across the floor and through a tiny technicians' room that linked the Art Room with Miss Temple's biology lab.

Mandy and James gave chase once more.

'There he is!' Mandy was first into the technicians' store. James followed and closed the door behind him. 'Up on that top shelf, see!'

The room was small and windowless. A fluorescent light showed them that Henry must have found the linking door that led into the biology lab closed. So, he'd climbed high and cornered himself near the ceiling, next to a stack of white cardboard boxes. Now he peered down at his pursuers, determined not to come down.

'Trust Vicki!' Mandy moaned, aware of the disturbance still going on in the Art Room. She didn't like the stuffy room with its smell of chemicals, its coils of rubber tubes, and its rows of brown bottles containing acid and poisonous crystals. 'If it hadn't been for her, we'd have got Henry safely back in his cage by now!'

'Shall I climb up and try to lift him down?' James asked. Henry had shifted along, almost knocking a box off the shelf.

Mandy nodded. 'Be careful, James!' With one eye on Henry and one on her friend, she held her breath.

'Here, Henry!' James climbed on to the worktop. He reached up. But his fingertips couldn't stretch far enough. The hamster shuffled further out of his grasp.

'Watch out!' Mandy cried.

Too late. This time the cardboard box shunted over the edge. It caught the empty jar on the next shelf, which toppled sideways, rolled, and dislodged a tall brown bottle, which in turn crashed to the floor and shattered.

James froze and listened to the splash of liquid. Mandy jumped quickly out of range. The sharp, strong fumes of acid caught in her throat. From his corner of the top shelf, Henry started in fear and vanished.

'Stay where you are!' Mandy told James. 'Don't tread on the floor, whatever you do! It's covered in broken glass and acid!'

'What about Henry?' James didn't move. 'If he touches it, that'll be the end!'

Mandy felt her mouth go dry. James was right. Poor Henry would be scared stiff and likely to do something reckless. Unless she got to him first, the chase could end in disaster. Fearfully she searched the cluttered shelves.

'Henry, don't be scared!' She began to whisper. Perhaps he would recognise the sound of her voice. 'It's all right, no one's going to hurt you!'

A little pink nose appeared from amongst the coils of rubber tube. It disappeared then came up again beside an old Bunsen burner. Henry's dark eyes stared at Mandy and his whole body trembled.

'That's a good boy. You know me, don't you? I'm not going to hurt you, I only want to take you out of this horrid place!' She eased closer, kneeling on a stool to keep her feet clear of the dangerous spillage. At last, her fingertips made contact with Henry's long, soft fur.

She felt him quiver, and heard the scratch of his claws on the shelf.

'There!' Softly she stroked him. 'Don't run away again. Let me pick you up!'

'Can you do it?' James whispered, still stranded on the worktop.

'I think so!' Mandy curled her fingers around Henry's warm body. His legs paddled against the shelf, then he gave up the struggle and nestled in her hands at last.

'He's still sleeping it off!' Miss Temple showed James and Mandy that Henry was curled up safe in his nest.

It was the end of school for the week. The technicians' room was spruce and clean again, and the hamster's trail of damage cleared up.

Mandy smiled at the sleeping form. Henry's cage was like a gym for hamsters, with ramps, galleries, and of course his exercise wheel. But he'd turned his back on them all. After his lunchtime on the run and a quick sponge-bath, he'd snoozed his way through the whole afternoon.

'About the reward, Miss Temple . . .' Mandy began. 'Well . . . James and I have discussed it, and, we were wondering . . . could we choose something different?'

'What did you have in mind?' Miss Temple asked.

'We wondered . . . that is, James and I would rather . . .' Mandy stammered over the request.

'Could we . . . maybe . . . ?' James did no better.

'I think I can guess what you want,' Miss Temple broke in. 'Did you want to take Henry home to Animal Ark for the weekend and look after him, by any chance?' She smiled. 'The answer is yes.'

'Really?' James's face broke into a wide grin.

'Thanks!' Mandy gasped. She glowed with pleasure, and pictured Henry at home, running up and down his ramps, with the exercise wheel going *treadle-treadle-treadle*! 'How did you guess?' she asked the teacher.

Henry stirred, blinked and opened his shiny eyes, then poked his nose out of his pile of paper and sniffed for food.

Miss Temple laughed out loud. 'It didn't take much doing, Mandy Hope. Remember, I know full well that both you and James are animal mad!'

*Read more about Henry's adventures in **Hamster in a Hamper**.*

Pony express!

'That's it, Prince,' Susan Collins said softly to her pony. 'Just take it gently and you'll get across.'

Prince, Susan's brown Welsh cob, stepped delicately into the rushing water of the stream. Susan could feel him tremble slightly. She laid a hand on his neck and settled deeper into the saddle, murmuring reassuringly to him. The water rose suddenly to the pony's hocks and he stopped.

'It's OK, Prince,' Susan whispered. 'This is as deep as it gets. Just watch out for the pebbles at the bottom.'

Prince raised his head and whickered. Susan was convinced the pony understood every word she said but she knew he wasn't happy.

Susan looked up briefly, glancing around the windswept moor. She and Prince were practising for the forthcoming county cross-country event and had been out all morning, negotiating the copses and hills and steep banks the ponies would have to master. Now it was time to try Prince out in running water – and Prince wasn't too keen on water.

Prince's head came up and he danced nervously, his hooves slipping on pebbles on the bed of the stream.

'Only a few more steps to go,' Susan encouraged. 'Look, Prince, you're nearly at the middle – almost halfway there!'

Prince's leading hoof skidded suddenly on the slippery pebbles and Susan adjusted her weight in the saddle. The water swirled and pulled at the pony's hocks. The stream was flowing a lot faster than usual because of the autumn storms. Prince's head came up and his eyes rolled towards her.

'Steady, Prince,' Susan soothed. 'Nearly there.'

Prince whickered again and he backed away from the turbulent water in midstream.

'Please, Prince,' Susan said softly. 'If you can't cross running water we won't be able to enter the cross-country event.'

But Prince had had enough. He wheeled and scrambled back up the bank, his hooves scrabbling for purchase on the wet and slippery mud. Then he was out of the water and standing on firm ground. Susan leaned over and rubbed his neck.

'It's OK, Prince,' she said comfortingly. 'I know you don't like it. We'll try again tomorrow. Maybe the water will be a bit calmer by then.'

'What's the problem, Susan?' called a voice.

Susan looked up and her mouth split into a wide smile. At the side of the road above her, Susan's friend, Mandy Hope, leaned out of the window of her father's Land-rover, looking concerned.

'Mandy!' Susan cried, giving the fair-haired girl a wave.

Mandy waved back and got out of the car. Adam Hope, Mandy's father, switched off the engine.

Up here, around the Yorkshire village of Welford, there were no fences separating the road from the moors. Susan and Prince cantered up to the side of the road.

'Hi, Mr Hope,' Susan said, smiling down at Mandy's dad. Adam Hope was a vet in Welford, and so was his wife, Mandy's mother, Emily Hope. Together they ran the Animal Ark veterinary practice.

'You looked as if you were having a bit of trouble there,' said Mr Hope.

Susan pulled a face. 'I can't get Prince to cross the stream,' she said. 'He's really good at all the other things we have to do for cross-country but if he can't cross water there's no point in entering.'

'That's a pity,' said Mandy. 'I was sure Prince would win a prize.' She ran a hand down Prince's neck and the pony whickered in response.

'I was just hoping we could get round the course,' Susan said. 'I'm concentrating really hard on crossing the streams at the moment. Prince isn't very keen on water so we're bound to lose time there even if I *can* get him to do it.'

'That's bad luck,' Mr Hope said. 'There's a lot of water about since those storms last week.'

'Isn't there anything Susan can do to help Prince, Dad?' Mandy asked. 'The cross-country is next week,' she pointed out. 'Susan and Prince don't have much time.'

Mr Hope looked thoughtful. 'She looks as if she's doing exactly the right thing already,' he said. 'The worst thing you can do with a frightened horse is force it, but getting over his fear could take a while.'

'I wouldn't force him,' Susan said. 'I'd rather forget the cross-country altogether than make Prince do anything he really doesn't want to do.' Susan leaned over and patted Prince's neck. 'We can enter next year,' she said. 'I'll keep on trying to get him ready for next week but Prince is more important than any cross-country event.'

'Good for you, Susan,' Mr Hope said. 'Take him gently and you'll succeed.'

'You can do it, Prince,' Mandy said firmly as she stroked the pony's neck. 'Even if you *do* have to wait until next year. What are his times like for the rest of the course, Susan?'

Susan shrugged. 'I haven't got round to timing him yet,' she said. 'I suppose I should but I'd have to ask somebody to come all the way up here to time me.'

Mandy grinned and looked at her father. 'Well, I'm here,' she said. 'I could time you if you like.'

'Would you?' said Susan. 'That would be great. But aren't you going somewhere?'

'We're just on our way home,' said Mr Hope. 'If you like, I can pick Mandy up in about an hour's time.'

Susan nodded enthusiastically. 'That would be great, Mr Hope. I'd really like to see how fast Prince can cover some of the ground.'

'OK, then,' Adam Hope said. 'But, Mandy, get your anorak out of the back. It looks like rain.'

Mandy opened the back door of the Land-rover and shifted her dad's bag to reach her anorak.

'Got it,' she said.

At that moment Mr Hope's mobile phone went off and he picked it up. Mandy and Susan watched as he listened, then spoke into it, his voice terse.

'Let me check,' he said. 'I think I've got some serum in my bag.'

'What is it, Dad?' asked Mandy anxiously.

Mr Hope looked worried. 'One of the cows at Twyford Farm is seriously ill,' he said. 'It's an emergency but we should be able to save it if I have the right serum with me.'

Adam Hope got out of the Land-rover and pulled his bag towards him, opening it. 'Got it!' he said, holding up a phial. 'Thank goodness for that.' He dropped the phial back in the bag and picked up the mobile again. 'I'm on my way, Tom,' he said. 'I've only got one phial of serum but that should be enough. I'm on the moor road and with any luck I'll be there in time. Meanwhile, try to keep the cow on her feet until I get there – and see if you can keep her temperature steady. I'll be as quick as I can.'

He turned to the girls. 'Got to go,' he said. 'Tom Hapwell is all on his own at Twyford. He's got his work cut out for him until I get there.'

Just then a lorry hurtled past on the road, throwing up a spray of water from its tyres. Prince danced nervously as the water splashed him. The pony bumped into Mr Hope as he swung his bag into the Land-rover. The bag dropped to the ground, spilling some of its contents. Mandy rushed to help her dad pick them up.

'Sorry, Mr Hope,' said Susan.

'It wasn't your fault,' Mr Hope reassured her. 'That lorry was going far too fast.'

Mr Hope swung the bag back into the Land-rover and got into the driver's seat. 'See you in an hour,' he said, as he revved the engine.

Susan and Mandy watched as the Land-rover disappeared swiftly down the moor road.

'I hope he gets there in time,' Mandy said.

Susan didn't say anything and Mandy looked at her. Susan was staring at the ground. She swung herself out of the saddle and bent down. 'Look, Mandy,' she said, picking something up and holding it out to her friend.

'It's the phial of serum,' Mandy said. 'It must have fallen out of Dad's bag and rolled under the Land-rover!'

'Your dad said it was the only one he had,' Susan said. 'What are we going to do? If he doesn't have this, he can't save the cow.'

'We could try and contact him on his mobile phone,' Mandy replied. 'But he'll be driving through Corran Dale, and the transmission is really bad,' she sighed. 'Even car radios don't work down there.'

Susan was keen to try anyway. 'Let's give it a go! There's a phone box on the roadside about half a kilometre away from here.'

'But, Susan,' said Mandy, frustrated, 'the real problem is that, even if we did manage to call Dad, he'd have to turn around and come all the way back here for the serum. And he'd never have time to turn back, then start the journey to Twyford Farm again.'

'You're right,' Susan sighed. 'He wasn't completely sure he would get there in time, anyway, even if he went straight there.'

'Maybe we could flag down a car,' said Mandy, desperately. 'Get somebody to take this to Twyford.'

Susan bit her lip and looked around. There wasn't a car in sight. 'There isn't much traffic on this road,' she said.

'So there's nothing we can do,' Mandy groaned, looking at the phial of serum in her hand. 'I just can't believe it. We've got the medicine to save a sick animal and there's nothing we can do to help.'

'Oh, yes there is,' said Susan.

Mandy looked at her. 'What?'

'Prince and I can take the phial and ride to Twyford Farm,' Susan replied.

'But it's miles,' said Mandy. 'You'd never get there in time. Even Dad was worried about getting there in time and he was driving.'

Susan shook her head. 'But he had to go by road,' she pointed out.

'What do you mean?' Mandy asked. 'What other way is there?'

Susan smiled. 'What do you think Prince and I have been practising for all month?' she asked.

Mandy's face lit up. 'Cross-country,' she said. 'You mean you'll go across the moors?'

Susan nodded. 'It'll cut the distance in half at least,' she said. 'It's worth a try.'

Mandy looked up at the sky. Clouds were gathering on the horizon and the first spots of rain had begun to fall.

'What about the weather?' she asked. 'It doesn't look too good. What if the mist comes down and you get lost on the moors?'

Susan looked serious. 'Look,' she said, 'it isn't as if nobody knows where I am. You know I'm out there, and that animal will die if it doesn't have that injection. There really isn't any choice, is there?'

Mandy hesitated. 'I suppose not,' she said. 'But don't do anything dangerous, Susan.'

Susan smiled, then leaped back on to Prince and stretched out her hand to Mandy. 'I'll drop you at the phone box on the way so you can let your dad know what's happening. Step on my foot and swing yourself up behind,' she instructed. 'Prince can carry us both for half a kilometre.'

Mandy reached out and took her friend's hand

firmly in her own, stepped lightly on Susan's braced foot, and then she was up on Prince, too.

'Poor Prince,' Mandy said. 'What a weight to carry.'

'He won't mind carrying you,' Susan replied. 'Prince has always liked you.' She clicked her tongue and Prince moved forward. 'Come on, Prince,' she urged. 'This is an emergency!'

Mandy was down and running for the phone box before Prince had even stopped moving. 'Just hang on, Susan,' she called, 'while I get you the phone box number, so you can call me when you get to the farm.'

A few seconds later Mandy gave Susan the number, scribbled on an old sweet wrapper, along with the precious phial of serum. 'Put it somewhere safe,' she said.

Susan grinned, took off her riding hat and slipped the phial under the inside band. 'There,' she replied. 'That's the safest place.'

'Be careful,' Mandy said. 'I'll try to get hold of Dad now – let him know you're on your way. Call as soon as you can.'

Susan smiled and swung herself into the saddle. The last thing she saw as she urged Prince off the road and on to the moor was Mandy's anxious face watching her. Then the drops of rain became heavier and she was out on the desolate moor with eight kilometres to ride across country to Twyford Farm. She was going to need all the skills she and Prince had learned in the past few months to make this journey. She hoped they were up to it – and that there wasn't a stream to cross!

Prince picked his way delicately across the moor. The mist was closing in, wrapping Susan in a cold damp blanket of fog. They were at the highest point on the moor now.

'Just let's get out of this mist and we'll be all right, Prince,' Susan whispered into her pony's ear.

She hoped her voice sounded more confident than she felt. At first the ride had been easy despite the increasing rain. Visibility hadn't been too bad, but Susan knew the shortest way to Twyford was up and over Highmoor Tor, and then the mist set in.

A white shape loomed out of the fog and Susan gasped – then laughed. It was only a sheep. 'If the sheep can find their way around the moor, so can you, Prince,' she said encouragingly.

Susan knew all about the mist on these moors. It could close in incredibly quickly, blotting everything from sight, leaving a walker or rider with no sense of direction. But it could clear just as swiftly. Susan crossed her fingers and hoped it would clear soon.

She peered into the mist. It seemed like a solid

object. Then she raised her head and tried to gauge their direction. Raindrops spattered on her upturned face, soaking through her shirt. She squared her shoulders. She couldn't sit here all day. She had to choose a direction and follow it.

'Come on, boy,' she urged Prince. 'We've got to get to Twyford.'

Susan tapped Prince lightly on the neck and he moved forward through the enveloping mist. Suddenly he stopped and Susan heard the splash of water.

'A stream, Prince,' she said, sliding off her pony's back. She peered down. 'It's just a little one. Don't worry. We won't cross it but if we follow it, it's bound to lead us down off the tor. I just hope we're headed in the right direction.'

Susan got back on Prince and touched her heels to his flank. Carefully, listening for the splash and tumble of water, she guided the pony downhill towards the lower slopes of Highmoor Tor and the flatter moorland beyond. Once down there perhaps the mist would lift.

It seemed like forever before they reached level ground. Suddenly the mist parted like a curtain and the sun came out. Susan stood in the stirrups, straining her eyes for landmarks, desperate to know if they had gone in the wrong direction.

With a sigh of relief she recognised the lie of the

land. A belt of trees beyond a small river showed her the boundary of Twyford Farm. A river, she thought. She'd forgotten about that river. She put it out of her mind. She and Prince would cope with that when they came to it.

'We've done it, Prince,' she shouted. 'There's Twyford. It can't be more than two kilometres away.'

Prince lifted his head and whinnied, glad to be out of the mist. Susan turned once. Highmoor Tor was still shrouded, but here the sun gleamed on the moorland, wet and sparkling from the rain.

She let out the reins and leaned over. 'Go for it, Prince!' she whispered in the pony's ear. 'There's no time to lose.'

Prince's ears came up, his tail flicked and he was off, racing across the springy turf, his long strides covering the ground, swallowing up the distance.

'We'll make it,' Susan cried joyfully, leaning forward, her body bent low over Prince's head.

Beneath her the pony moved like the wind, his mane flying. Then Susan saw the river up ahead and felt Prince's strides falter beneath her. 'Oh, no,' she said. 'Look at it!'

Prince skidded to a stop only a metre from the bank of the river. Susan looked down at the swollen torrent. The water was muddy brown, swirling downstream, splashing high against its banks. Prince stood rigid.

'Come on, boy,' Susan pleaded. 'It's not so bad. Try it – for me.'

But Prince's eyes rolled. He didn't like water much – and he especially didn't like this.

Susan bit her lip. Across the river were the trees and beyond that Twyford Farm. It was less than half a kilometre away and she couldn't get there. She thought of Mr Hope finding out he had lost the serum, of Mandy waiting by the telephone for news and of Tom Hapwell and the sick cow. She *must* get there! She had to – even if she had to swim to do it.

Making up her mind, Susan leapt down from the pony's back and hung the reins over his head.

'Stay there,' she said. 'I'll come back for you.'

Warily she put one foot in the swirling waters of the river. The strength of the water tugged at her riding boot. She clamped her lips together as a tendril of fear invaded her mind. This river wasn't deep, she told herself. She'd paddled in it loads of times. Even with the extra water in it she should still be able to wade across.

Doggedly she lifted her other foot and stepped out towards the middle of the river. At once the water covered her riding boots and began to seep into them. She gasped. The water was cold. It was also flowing much faster out here in the middle of the river than she had thought. Below the surface, the cross currents

churned around her legs, pulling her off balance.
Suddenly Susan was very frightened. She had mis-
judged the situation badly. Prince had been right. The
river *was* dangerous!

She tried to turn to make her way back to the safety
of the bank but the current dragged at her legs, and
the stones beneath her feet felt slippery and unsafe.
She stumbled and cried out.

There was an answering call from the river bank.
At first she thought it was a person. Then she realised
it was Prince whinnying, his head tossing.

Susan turned clumsily and her foot slipped. She tried
to recover her balance but the water rushing past her
legs, dragging at her feet, made her feel dizzy. With a
cry of terror, she tumbled head-first into the water.

Struggling against panic, she tried to raise herself
but her foot slipped again and this time she felt the
current toss her forwards, rolling her over. She cried
out, lifting her hands, trying to catch hold of something – anything. But there was nothing to grab. Water
poured around her face, taking her breath away. She
surfaced, frantically gasping for air, too breathless
even to cry out.

She heard the drum of hooves on grass then a splash
and, seconds later, there *was* something to hold on
to. Prince had plunged into the swirling water after
her.

Susan reached desperately for his bridle and hung on, gasping, trying to get her breath back. The pony stood there, rock solid in the churning water. He turned his head and she managed to speak.

'Oh, Prince. You've come to rescue me. Oh, thank you boy!'

Prince gave a whicker and began to move forward, his strong legs surging through the water. Susan clung on to his bridle and hauled herself up, using the pony to steady herself.

Prince scrambled up the bank and they both stood there for a moment, shivering but safe.

Susan threw her arms round her pony's neck. Her legs felt weak and she was chilled to the bone – but she still had a job to do.

'Brave boy,' she said, her teeth chattering.

Carefully, she took off her hat, and her dark brown hair tumbled around her shoulders in wet strands. 'It's still there,' she said with relief, looking at the unbroken phial. She put her hat back on her head, the phial still securely tucked underneath it. 'Now let's really gallop for Twyford, Prince,' she said. 'I'm frozen stiff.'

'What on earth is going on?' said Mr Hope as Susan came flying up the farm track on Prince.

Susan drew the pony to a halt and leaped down, dragging off her riding hat.

'I've got it,' she said breathlessly. 'I've got the serum. It fell out of your bag.'

'I've been looking for it everywhere,' said Mr Hope. 'Where did you find it? No, don't bother. There isn't time. You can tell me later – but thanks, Susan.'

Mr Hope turned to Tom Hapwell. 'I don't quite understand this,' he said, 'but it looks like we can save that cow after all. Come on, Tom.'

'You'd better get inside and get dried off,' Tom said to Susan as he turned to follow Mr Hope into the barn. 'I don't know what you've been up to but I guess that there are a few thanks in order from me too.'

Susan grinned. 'I'm nearly dry already,' she said. 'But I wouldn't mind emptying my boots out.'

Mr Hope gave her a look over his shoulder, then said, 'You look half-drowned, but the explanation can wait. I'll see to the cow first.'

Susan sighed with relief. The transmission in Corran Dale must have been too bad for Mandy to have been able to make phone contact with her father after all, but everything would be OK now.

Ten minutes later, Mr Hope and Tom walked out into the farmyard.

'How is the cow?' asked Susan.

Tom Hapwell smiled. 'Looking great,' he said. 'That injection really did the trick.'

Susan was rubbing Prince down. 'Did you hear that, Prince?' she said. 'You saved the cow.'

Prince whinnied as if he understood what she said and nuzzled her neck.

'What on earth have you got on your feet, Susan?' asked Mr Hope. Susan looked down at her feet. They were encased in a huge pair of checked carpet slippers.

'My boots are drying on the Aga,' she said cheerfully. 'I borrowed these. I hope you don't mind, Mr Hapwell.'

Tom Hapwell shook his head. 'You're welcome,' he said. 'Now, what on earth have you been up to?'

Susan explained. '. . . So Prince waded into the river to rescue me,' she finished.

Adam Hope looked concerned. 'That river isn't usually very deep,' he said.

Susan nodded. 'That's what I thought,' she replied. 'I didn't realise how strong the current would be after the storms. If it hadn't been for Prince I might have drowned. He just plunged in after me. Wasn't he brave?'

'He certainly was,' said Mr Hope. 'Especially for a pony who doesn't like running water. That might just have done the trick as far as his fear of water is concerned.'

Susan's eyes grew round. 'Oh, I hadn't thought of that,' she said. Her eyes were shining. 'Do you think he's cured? Do you think he'll be OK crossing water from now on?'

'I think there's every chance,' said Adam Hope. 'He didn't think about his own fear when he went in after you. I don't think Prince will let you go anywhere near water on your own again.'

'Wow!' said Susan. 'Wait till I tell Mandy.' She put her hand to her mouth. 'Oops, I said I'd phone her at the telephone box on the moor road. I'd better go and do that.' She made a dash for the farmhouse, her borrowed slippers flapping.

'Tell her I'll be right over to pick her up,' Adam Hope called after her.

Susan grinned as she sped into the house and punched out the telephone box numbers. The paper was a bit soggy.

'Did it,' she said as Mandy picked up the phone. 'The serum was delivered by pony express and the cow is all right.'

'Great! Well done!' said Mandy. 'But what about you? The mist came down so suddenly I was afraid you'd get lost.'

'Well,' Susan said, 'you'll never guess what happened . . .'

Read more about Prince's adventures in **Pony in the Porch**.

That horror Houdini!

'But I don't even *like* Imogen Parker Smythe,' Amy Fawcett said plaintively to her aunt. She pushed her curly dark hair out of her eyes and looked mutinous. 'You should have heard what she said about High Cross Farm when I met her in the lane the other day.'

'What did she say?' asked Lydia Fawcett, opening a sack of feed for her goats.

'She said High Cross was a tip and it should be knocked down,' said Amy, outraged. 'That's Imogen Parker Smythe for you!'

'She's only seven,' said Lydia reasonably.

'Yes, but she's nearly as big a snob as her mother,' said Amy. 'I don't want to go to her stuck-up party.'

Lydia Fawcett looked up from tipping feed into Houdini the goat's trough. 'It's her birthday,' she said. 'Mrs Parker Smythe particularly asked if you could come to her party. Imogen doesn't have many friends.'

'I'm not surprised,' Amy said, stroking Houdini's nose. 'Imogen is *so* spoiled. She gets everything she wants. And she thinks she's great just because her parents are so well off.'

'Not like us,' said Lydia, standing up and running a hand through her untidy grey hair.

The Parker Smythes lived in a huge modern house on Beacon Hill not far from High Cross, Lydia's goat farm. Lydia Fawcett just managed to make a living out of selling goat's milk and cheese. High Cross was anything but posh but Amy loved it.

'I'd rather stay here with you and Houdini and the other goats than go to a fancy party any day,' Amy said firmly. 'Wouldn't I, Houdini?'

The black and white billy goat nuzzled Amy's hand and she laughed. Amy had come to stay with her aunt for the summer while her parents were abroad. She adored Lydia's goats, especially Houdini. He followed her everywhere and the two had become firm friends.

'Mrs Parker Smythe said Jasper is going to be at the party too,' said Aunt Lydia.

'Who's Jasper?' asked Amy, scratching Houdini

under the chin. She screwed up her face. 'What a name!'

'Jasper is Imogen's cousin,' Aunt Lydia replied. 'He goes to boarding school. That's why you haven't met him before. He's visiting for the holidays. He's eleven, like you.'

'Jasper!' said Amy. 'He sounds even worse than Imogen.'

Lydia Fawcett looked worried. 'I thought you might like to go to a party and meet some other young people,' she said. 'It would be nice if you made some friends in Welford while you're visiting. After all, you're going to be here all summer.'

'But what about all that cheese you've got to package?' Amy said. 'I was going to help you with it.'

Lydia's main problem recently had been packaging her cheeses. It took ages and Lydia wasn't very good at it.

'Oh, I can manage for one afternoon,' said Lydia. 'But if you really don't want to go I'll ring and say you can't come.' She sighed. 'Mrs Parker Smythe put in a big order for goat's cheese when she phoned about the party. I hope she won't cancel it now.'

Amy bit her lip. Lydia worked so hard rearing her goats, making cheese and selling goat's milk. Losing even one order would make a difference to her. Amy made up her mind. Aunt Lydia's business was much more important to Amy than being bored for an afternoon at a posh party.

'No, don't do that, Aunt Lydia,' she said. 'You've promised, and Mrs Parker Smythe probably *would* cancel her order. I'll go to the party – but I don't expect I'll enjoy it much.' She looked at Houdini. 'I wish you'd been invited, Houdini,' she said. 'Then I wouldn't mind going.'

Lydia laughed. 'Can you imagine Houdini at a garden party?' she said. 'Mrs Parker Smythe would have a fit.'

Amy giggled. 'Do you know what she called Houdini last week?'

Lydia shook her head. 'Do I really want to know?' she asked.

Amy grinned. 'I was taking Houdini for a walk down the lane and Mrs Parker Smythe passed in her car with Imogen,' she said. 'They stopped for a minute and Houdini began to nibble on the car tyres. "Get that horror Houdini away from the car!" Mrs Parker Smythe yelled. What a cheek! "That horror Houdini"!'

'I'm afraid Mrs Parker Smythe doesn't like goats much,' said Lydia.

'Hmmph!' Amy said. 'Some people have no *taste*!'

'Have you tried the go-karts yet, dear?' Mrs Parker Smythe said to Amy.

Amy shook her head. 'Not yet, Mrs Parker Smythe.'

'Do try them, dear,' Mrs Parker Smythe said. 'They cost a *fortune* to hire. I do hope they don't make too much mess on the drive. If any of them run over my herbaceous border I'll have something to say. That border has won prizes you know!'

'Oh, the gardener will fix all that, Mummy,' Imogen said, her round face looking smug. 'I've just had my picture taken for the local paper.'

'Really?' said Mrs Parker Smythe, patting her bright blonde hair. The bangles on her wrist jangled and her earrings clinked. Mrs Parker Smythe always wore lots of jewellery.

'Come and have another photograph taken with me,' she said to Imogen. 'A mother and daughter picture is so sweet, I always think.'

Mrs Parker Smythe walked off with Imogen in tow and Amy looked around the garden at Beacon House in disbelief. 'Some garden party!' she muttered.

It was more like a funfair. In addition to the go-karts on the driveway there was a carousel set up on the lawn, a magician doing tricks in a tent and a huge inflatable raft floating in the indoor swimming pool.

'It's awful, isn't it?' said a voice beside her. 'Really over the top.'

Amy looked round. A boy with straight fair hair was standing beside her, his hands stuffed in his pockets. He looked really fed up.

'Why can't Imogen just have a party like everybody else?' Amy said. 'You know, cake and ice cream and proper party games?'

The boy nodded. 'That's what I said,' he replied, kicking at the gravel of the drive moodily. 'This is really embarrassing. I'm glad none of *my* friends are here.'

Amy looked puzzled. 'Embarrassing?' she said.

The boy nodded. 'My aunt always overdoes things,' he said.

Amy swallowed, wondering if she had put her foot in it. 'You must be Jasper,' she said.

'That's right, but call me Jass,' said the boy. 'Everybody does – except my aunt. Who are you?'

'Amy Fawcett,' said Amy. 'I'm staying with *my* aunt at High Cross for the summer.'

Jass's face lit up. 'The goat farm?' he said. 'Lucky you.'

Amy smiled. 'You're not a bit like Imogen,' she said. 'Do you like goats?'

'I like all animals,' Jass said. 'Goats included.'

'Come up to High Cross some time,' said Amy. 'You can give us a hand.'

'Looking after the goats?' said Jass. 'I'd love that.'

'Packing cheese as well,' Amy said. 'That's a real chore.'

Jass grinned. 'You should talk to my uncle about that,' he said. 'That's where he made all his money. He invented this really cool packaging system and it took off. He made pots of money. Then he went into satellite TV.'

'You mean he hasn't always been rich?' said Amy.

Jass shook his head. 'Oh, no,' he said. 'My aunt and uncle used to be perfectly normal.'

Amy grinned. Jass was OK.

'So, what do you want to do?' said Jass.

'I'd *really* like to be at High Cross with Houdini,' Amy said.

'Who's Houdini?' said Jass.

'My favourite goat,' said Amy.

'Maybe we could escape and do that,' said Jass.

Amy giggled. 'Houdini is the expert at escaping,' she said. 'That's how he got his name. Years and years ago there was an escapologist called Houdini. He could get out of anything. So can my Houdini.'

'He sounds great,' said Jass. 'So what are we waiting for? Let's go!'

There was a snort from a nearby bush and Amy looked around. A long black and white face appeared, munching on the bush.

'Too late!' she said. '*That's* Houdini.'

'Wow!' said Jass. 'He must have followed you here.'

'He follows me everywhere,' said Amy, moving

towards the bush. 'Houdini!' she breathed. 'What on earth are you doing here?'

The goat looked at her, sprigs of greenery hanging out of the corners of his mouth.

'Another of your escaping tricks!' Amy said severely to him.

As she watched, Houdini stepped delicately out from behind the bush and lowered his head towards Mrs Parker Smythe's prize herbaceous border. There was a tearing sound as his strong teeth ripped up a mouthful of blooms.

'Oh, Houdini,' Jass said, looking around. 'Come out of there. My aunt will have a thousand fits if she sees what you're doing to her plants – her *prize* herbaceous border!'

Houdini ripped up another clump of flowers and Amy giggled. 'Come on!' she said. 'Let's get you out of here.'

Houdini gave a snort and Amy looked around. There at the end of the path were Imogen and her mother. Mrs Parker Smythe was gathering up all the children and herding them towards the big marquee on the lawn.

'Time for the magician,' she was saying in a piercing voice. 'Come and see the tricks!'

'Uh-oh!' said Jass to Houdini. 'Let's hope she doesn't see the tricks you've been up to, Houdini.'

'What are we going to do?' said Amy.

'Hide him until the coast is clear,' Jass said, thinking quickly. 'I know. We'll put him in the garden room. He can't do much damage there.'

Everybody else was making for the marquee. With any luck they would get Houdini out of sight before Mrs Parker Smythe saw him. Amy grabbed Houdini's collar and tried to drag him towards the house. Houdini stiffened his back legs and resisted.

'Please, Houdini,' Amy pleaded. 'We'll get into terrible trouble if Mrs Parker Smythe finds you. She'll never buy any of Aunt Lydia's cheese again!'

Houdini put his head on one side and whickered but he didn't move.

'Try this,' said Jass. He grabbed a handful of flowers and held it out in front of the goat's nose. 'Come on, boy!' he said.

Amy could hear Mrs Parker Smythe's voice in the distance. 'Jasper!' she called. 'Where *have* you got to now?'

'This way,' said Jass, walking backwards and holding the flowers just out of Houdini's reach. 'There's a side door to the garden room.'

Amy guided Houdini towards the house. Jass swung open the side door and Amy thrust the goat through and out of sight. Jass tossed the flowers in after him, shut the door and leaned against it just as Mrs Parker

Smythe appeared round the corner of the house.

'There you are, Jasper,' Mrs Parker Smythe said. 'Come along now. We can't keep the magician waiting. You too, Amy.' With that, she turned on her heel and marched off.

'We'd better go,' said Jass.

Amy opened the door a crack and a black and white muzzle thrust itself into her hand.

'Be good, Houdini,' she whispered. 'I'll be back as soon as I can.'

'Jasper!' shouted Mrs Parker Smythe.

'Coming,' Jass called back. Amy shut the door and crossed her fingers. She just hoped Houdini wouldn't escape again – but, knowing Houdini, she wouldn't bet on it!

'Wonderful!' said Mrs Parker Smythe at the end of the magician's performance. 'Now I've got a treat for all of you – in the garden room.'

Amy gasped. The garden room! That was where they had put Houdini. She looked at Jass in horror.

'Can't we have just one more trick?' she said to Mrs Parker Smythe. She hoped that if the magician did one more trick they could manage to slip away and get Houdini out of the garden room.

Imogen's mother looked down her nose at Amy. 'There's no time,' she said. 'We've got a programme to follow and I want you all to enjoy yourselves. We're going to sing "Happy Birthday" and cut Imogen's birthday cake and you'll all have a great big slice of it.'

Amy's heart sank. As if things weren't bad enough, now she had locked Houdini in a room with a birthday cake in it. She didn't give much for the cake's chances with Houdini around.

'Nobody told me they were putting the cake in the garden room,' Jass said mournfully.

'You did your best, Jass,' Amy said. 'Thanks for the help.'

'It didn't do much good, did it?' said Jass.

Dismally they trooped after Mrs Parker Smythe and the others.

'Maybe if I cut across the lawn I could get to the garden room first,' said Amy.

She was just about to make a dash for it when Mrs Parker Smythe screeched.

'WHAT is that?' she yelled, clutching her throat and pointing at the garden room window.

A long black and white face peered out of the window at them. There was a pink candle hanging out of the side of Houdini's mouth. As Mrs Parker Smythe watched, horrified, Houdini calmly chomped up the candle.

Amy flapped her hands wildly. 'Get down, Houdini,' she said before she could stop herself.

Mrs Parker Smythe whirled on her. 'HOUDINI!' she roared. 'You brought that horror to Beacon House! You brought a *goat* to my darling's birthday party!'

'She didn't exactly *bring* him,' Jass said helpfully, but his aunt's eyes were fixed on Amy.

Amy flinched. Several of the others had crowded round the window, peering in.

'Oh, isn't he nice?' one of them said.

'Nice!' yelled Mrs Parker Smythe. 'He's a monster!' Her eyes fell on the prize herbaceous border just outside the garden room. 'Look at that!' she yelled. 'I don't need to ask who did that. Wait till I get my hands on that goat!'

Imogen turned from the window, her face streaked with tears. 'It's eaten my birthday cake!' she wailed.

Mrs Parker Smythe drew herself up and marched towards the garden room door. 'Don't you worry, my pet,' she said to Imogen. 'It's the last birthday cake that animal will ever eat.' And with that, she wrenched open the garden room door.

Amy dashed past her, flinging her arms across the doorway.

'It isn't Houdini's fault,' she said. 'He can't help it. What are you going to do to him?'

Mrs Parker Smythe drew breath and, just at that moment, the door on the other side of the room opened and Mr Parker Smythe appeared.

'Good heavens, what's happened here?' he said.

Amy whirled round as Mr Parker Smythe came forward, peering at Houdini.

Houdini took to his heels and raced out, past Mr Parker Smythe. Amy and Jass made a dive for the door.

'Come back!' Mrs Parker Smythe shouted. But Amy wasn't listening. All she wanted was to get hold of Houdini and protect him from Mrs Parker Smythe.

'No, Houdini,' she yelled as she saw the goat make for the stairs.

Too late. Houdini was up the stairs and out of sight before Amy had even put a foot on the first step.

Amy and Jass charged upstairs with Mr and Mrs Parker Smythe, Imogen and the rest of the partygoers behind them.

There were a lot of doors leading off the corridor at the top of the stairs – but only one was open.

'Uh-oh, that's my aunt's bedroom,' Jass said.

Amy bit her lip. She only hoped there was another way out of the room. As she charged towards the open door she heard a yell and a thump from inside.

'Oh, no,' she muttered. 'What now?'

Amy and Jass hurtled through the door, everyone else hard on their heels. Amy stopped suddenly and all the others ran into her. There, in the middle of the room, was Houdini – sitting on top of a dark-haired man.

The man swivelled his eyes. 'Get this thing off me,' he yelled.

Mrs Parker Smythe took a step forward, brushing Amy out of the way and almost knocking the breath out of her.

'And who might you be?' she said to the man on the floor, her voice rising.

Amy pointed, almost unable to speak. 'Look!' she squeaked.

Mrs Parker Smythe peered at the man's hands. He was clutching a bundle of glittering necklaces. As he tried to get out from under Houdini, several brooches and earrings rolled on to the floor and lay there sparkling.

'My jewellery!' Mrs Parker Smythe screeched. 'Thief! Call the police!'

Mr Parker Smythe reached for the phone by the bed and Houdini regarded the fallen earrings with interest. He made a move towards them but Amy was quicker. Swiftly she dived, gathering up the jewels. 'No, Houdini,' she said. 'The flowers and the birthday cake were bad enough. You can't eat Mrs Parker Smythe's earrings!'

'Don't let that goat move until the police arrive, Jass,' Mr Parker Smythe said as he put down the phone.

'What?' said Mrs Parker Smythe to her husband. 'You're not going to let that horrible animal stay here, are you?'

'That horrible animal saved your jewellery,' Jass said.

Mrs Parker Smythe looked bewildered for a moment. Then she smiled. 'Of course he did,' she said.

She strode over to a cut glass vase of flowers, lifted the whole bunch out and walked over to Houdini, holding it out for him.

'There, there. Good boy,' she said. 'Just you stay where you are until help arrives.'

Amy's eyes widened in astonishment. Houdini was still sitting on the man on the floor. Mrs Parker Smythe looked at the burglar.

'If you try to move,' she said. 'I'll get Houdini to bite you. That goat will eat anything. Isn't that right, Amy?'

Amy gulped. Now Mrs Parker Smythe was cooing over the goat, stroking him.

'My lovely jewels,' she said. 'You've saved my jewels, Houdini. What a wonderful goat you are.' She turned to Amy. 'How can I ever thank you?' she said.

Jass walked over to his uncle and whispered in his ear. Mr Parker Smythe smiled.

'I think Jass has just thought of a way,' he said.

Amy looked enquiringly at Jass but he just grinned. She didn't care. She was just happy things had turned out all right.

'One more, please,' said the photographer from the local paper. 'This time can we have the goat right in the middle of the picture? This is going to make a great story. Can you hold that necklace up just a little bit, Mrs Parker Smythe?'

It was the end of the party. The police had taken the burglar away and Mrs Parker Smythe looked as if she was wearing every single bit of her jewellery.

'You know, I'm really glad you came to Imogen's party,' Jass said to Amy.

Amy grinned. 'I told Aunt Lydia it would be really boring,' she said, laughing. '*Boring*!'

'Did you mean it when you said I could come up to High Cross and help out?' said Jass.

Amy nodded. 'I hope you don't mind packing cheese,' she said.

'Oh, you don't have to worry about that any longer,' said Jass.

Amy looked at him, surprised. 'Why not?' she said.

'Because I told my uncle that as a reward he should send one of his old packaging machines up to High Cross,' said Jass. 'Your Aunt Lydia won't have to do it all by hand any more.'

'That's great,' said Amy. 'Thanks, Jass!'

'Smile, please,' said the photographer.

Amy smiled. She had plenty to smile about. She had a new friend and a great surprise for Aunt Lydia – and Houdini wasn't a horror to Mrs Parker Smythe any more!

Read more about Houdini's adventures in **Goat in the Garden**.

Bravo, Blackie!

'I'm really sorry,' Mandy said to James when he rang to see if she wanted to take Blackie on a training session. 'I'm going into Walton with Mum.'

'Oh . . . OK. I'll see you soon.' James felt disappointed as he put the phone down. Their obedience training with Blackie was always great fun. 'Well, Blackie,' he said to the Labrador, 'it looks like we'll have to go on our own.'

James and Mandy had been training the young dog for ages. Labrador Retrievers were supposed to retrieve and James was determined that's what Blackie should do. Unfortunately, they weren't having much luck. Blackie was excellent at running after things but not very good at bringing them back.

There was a cold wind blowing as James walked with Blackie across the village green. The sky was grey and the air had a feel of winter. It was late autumn and the ground was covered with a carpet of golden leaves. James kicked through them as he headed for the narrow lane that led to Millers Pond.

He had decided he would try to get Blackie to bring back sticks he had thrown into the water. Blackie was a brilliant swimmer. He splashed through puddles, dived into streams, plunged into lakes. In fact, water was his favourite thing of all.

'Right, Blackie,' James said, when they reached the pond. He kicked around in the grass, looking for a stick to throw. The surface of the pond was rippled by the wind and even the ducks had taken refuge in the reeds.

Mandy and James often went there to watch the wildlife: ducks, moorhens, herons and dragonflies all flitted across the surface. Once they had spotted a kingfisher darting to and fro, busily building its nest in the muddy bank. But there was no such activity today. Nest-building had finished months ago. All the nestlings had grown up and gone. James knew now that Blackie splashing around in the water wouldn't disturb any of the wild creatures that had made the pond their home.

'Right.' James found a long stick and broke it in half. Blackie sat expectantly at his feet. His tongue lolled and his eyes were bright with excitement. This was exactly the sort of game he loved. Getting a stick and running off with it . . . or in this case, swimming off with it, then refusing to bring it back. Excellent!

James threw it as far as he could. 'Fetch!' he shouted.

There was a loud splash as Blackie plunged reck-lessly in and swam after the stick. Through the reeds, ploughing through tangles of waterweed, his black head was just visible above the surface. He grabbed the stick, turned and swam back towards James.

James jumped up and down. Blackie was really retrieving a stick. Wait until he told Mandy! 'Good boy!' he shouted. 'Bring it here . . . good boy!'

But his jubilation was short-lived. Blackie obviously had other ideas. He turned again and swam back towards the middle. If James thought he was going to give up the stick so easily he had another think coming.

On the bank, James was trying not to get annoyed. He had a book on dog training. '*Always call in a kind voice,*' it said. '*If you scold a dog he will never come back to you.*'

James swallowed and tried to keep calm. 'Blackie . . . bring it here . . . good boy!'

Blackie ignored him.

'Oh dear.' James sighed, and tutted. It was really hard not to get angry but he knew it would be the wrong thing to do.

Suddenly he heard the sound of laughter and turned to see a boy of about seven or eight standing watching Blackie's antics. He had a small brown puppy on a lead. The puppy didn't seem to like being restrained and was growling and trying to bite the end of the lead.

'Your dog's not very good, is he?' the boy said.

'Well,' James grinned. 'He's very good at running after things . . . he just won't bring them back.'

He crouched down to stroke the puppy. 'What's his name?' he asked.

'Stumpy,' the boy told him. 'We've only just got him. He's a terrier cross.'

The little dog wagged his long tail at James and tried to nibble at his fingers.

'Is he good?' James asked.

The boy shook his head. 'Not yet, but Mum says he will be when we've trained him.'

James grinned again. 'Well, I hope you have more luck than me.'

By now, Blackie had reached the far bank, clambered out of the water and was shaking himself. Then he picked up the stick again and ran off into the corn stubble. A pheasant flew up, squawking in fear, its cry echoing across the water.

'Blackie!' Now James *was* getting annoyed. Blackie was definitely *not* allowed to chase pheasants.

Blackie must have known, because he turned and headed back towards James and the boy. As he reached them James grabbed the stick. 'Leave!' he commanded.

But Blackie growled and shook his head and hung on to it for dear life.

'Blackie . . . leave!'

Blackie let it go. He gave James a look that seemed to say *sorry*, then began sniffing round the puppy, his tail waving enthusiastically. The puppy's tail wagged nineteen to the dozen too as he rolled over on his back and let Blackie sniff him.

'Hey, Stumpy, you try!'

Suddenly, before James could stop him, the boy dropped the puppy's lead, picked up another stick and threw it into the water as hard as he could.

The puppy rolled on to his feet, ears pricked. Then he lunged forward and plunged headlong into the water. Blackie ran forward and into the water too.

James felt a pang of fear. It was OK for Blackie to swim – he was a fine, strong dog. But for a little puppy . . . it was really dangerous.

Beside him, the little boy was jumping up and down with excitement. 'Go on, Stumpy, fetch it, there's a good boy!'

The puppy struggled but his lead had become soaked with water and seemed to be dragging him down. Blackie had reached the stick and was swimming off with it in the opposite direction.

The boy was still encouraging his dog. 'Come on, Stumpy . . . come back now.'

But the little dog was too young even to know his name. He swam round and round, his little paws barely splashing the water. Then, suddenly, his lead became tangled up in the weeds and his head went under.

'Stumpy!' The little boy was screaming with fear now. 'He's drowning! Stumpy!' He looked at James, his eyes wide with fright. 'Please get him for me, I can't swim.'

James's heart was beating like a drum. He couldn't just stand there and watch the little dog drown. But he knew how treacherous it would be to plunge into the water. Maybe if he just *waded* in . . . ?

He wrenched off his coat. 'I'll see if I can get him.' He bent rapidly to undo the laces of his trainers.

By now, Blackie was standing on the far bank, dripping with water. He looked at James as if he was expecting to be scolded. When it was obvious James wasn't going to call him back he sniffed around in the rushes for a moment or two then began ambling back.

James was already thigh-deep in the water. He

shuddered as he felt the cold water seep through his jeans. The bottom of the pond was muddy; he could feel it oozing up between his toes. His eyes scanned the surface anxiously. The puppy had been struggling desperately but now there was no sign of him; just a few bubbles, a few ripples, where he had been. Nothing more.

The little boy was still screaming when all of a sudden a man appeared from the trees. 'Ian . . . what on earth's wrong?' It was his dad, who'd come to see what he was up to.

Ian pointed frantically. 'Stumpy's in the water. He can't swim. That boy's looking for him.'

'Hey!' Ian's dad called. 'Come out, it's dangerous! Let me have a go.'

'It's OK,' James shouted as he waded further out. There didn't seem to be much point in two people getting soaked. But he had a feeling it wasn't going to do any good. Even if he dived down he'd never find the little dog. It was murky and dark . . . too dark to see anything. James's eyes scanned the surface frantically. No sign . . . Stumpy had gone.

Ian's dad was still shouting from the bank. 'For goodness sake be careful!'

James thought this was turning out to be the very worst day of his life.

Then suddenly Stumpy's head bobbed above the

surface. The lead had come loose and he was free again. For a few seconds, his little paws paddled like mad as he tried to swim.

'Here!' James gasped. 'Stumpy! Here.'

But by now Stumpy was very weak. He was shivering with cold and had taken in a lot of water.

Suddenly there was a loud bark from the bank and a huge splash. Blackie had plunged into the water. He was soon beside James, swimming strongly towards the struggling puppy.

'Good boy!' James panted. He pointed. 'Fetch! Good boy!'

The exhausted puppy had disappeared under the surface again and for a moment, James couldn't see anything. Blackie went down under the water. There was a heart-stopping moment when James couldn't see either dog. Then Blackie surfaced. He had something grasped in his mouth. It was the puppy. Blackie turned and swam towards James.

'Good boy! This way!' James yelled as he waded backwards, through the mud, the water-weed and the rushes that grew by the bank. For the first time in his life Blackie followed obediently.

Ian and his father were shouting encouragement from the bank. 'Blackie, come on . . . come *on*!'

The Labrador had the puppy gently by the scruff of his neck, just as a mother dog would do with her

pups as she carried them from one place to another.

James's heart thumped with excitement. He hardly noticed how cold and shivery he felt, or how wet and muddy his clothes were. All he could think of was that, at last, Blackie was doing as he was told.

James, Blackie and the puppy were all soon on dry land. Blackie deposited Stumpy at James's feet. He shook himself then looked up at him with big brown eyes. James didn't know how he managed not to cry as he bent and gave his dog a huge hug.

'Blackie, you're totally brilliant,' he said. He rubbed the dog's chest. 'Good dog!' Blackie's tail wagged so quickly it was just a blur.

Ian and his father came running towards them. 'Is Stumpy OK?' the man asked anxiously.

It was then that James noticed that the little puppy wasn't moving. It lay at his feet, a soaked, matted, motionless bundle of fur.

Ian bent down, sobbing. 'He's dead!'

Blackie sniffed the little animal. Then he began licking him frantically as if his big red tongue would bring the puppy back to life. James picked up the little dog and ran to where his jacket was lying on the bank. He had suddenly remembered a programme he had seen on TV where a fireman rescued a kitten from a burning building. The kitten seemed to be dead but when the fireman breathed into its mouth it came round.

James quickly wrapped the little dog in his coat. He opened the puppy's jaw and bent his head towards him. Then he breathed into its mouth, soft, blowing breaths.

Please let him be all right . . . please let him be all right, James prayed silently to himself. The little boy would be heartbroken if the pup really was dead.

It seemed to James that the whole world was standing still as he tried to revive Stumpy. Blackie sat watching, panting softly, his coat gleaming with water. It was as if he knew the little dog was hovering between life and death.

Ian and his father were crouched beside James. Ian was crying softly.

The wind had dropped and there was no sound other than the soft hissing of James's breath. In . . . out . . . in . . . out.

Then suddenly Ian gave a gasp. The puppy was moving. First one leg twitched, then another. He stirred and opened his eyes. James rubbed him gently with his coat to warm him, to get his blood circulation going. Then he bent and breathed again.

The puppy wriggled in his hands.

Still cradled in the coat, James handed him to Ian with a sigh of relief. 'There you are, he should be fine now, although I would take him to Animal Ark for a check-up, if I were you.'

'Oh, *thank you*!' Ian's eyes were shining as he hugged his puppy to his chest.

Ian's dad shook James's hand. 'Thanks, son, that was wonderful. And your dog . . . how on earth did you train him to do that?'

James looked at Ian and gave him a wink. 'Oh,' he said. 'Just patience really.'

By now James was shivering with cold. His jeans were sodden and muddy, his sweatshirt soaked.

'You'd better get home before you catch your death,' Ian's father said when he had asked James his name and where he lived. He finished jotting it down in a notebook he had taken from his pocket. 'And thanks again.' He patted Blackie's head. 'Great dog you've got there.'

'You and I are going to be in trouble,' James said to Blackie as they both ran along the high street and across the green towards home.

His mum wouldn't be at all pleased that his best pair of jeans and his trainers were caked with mud. Blackie would need a bath too. He stank of mud and pond water.

Later, Mandy phoned. 'We're back,' she said. 'Want to go training with Blackie now?'

But James didn't really feel like it. Luckily, his mum had been out when he and Blackie had arrived home. He had sponged off the worst of the mud from his jeans and sweatshirt and put them into the dirty linen basket. Hopefully his mum would put them into the washing machine without looking at them too closely. He'd tried his best to clean up his trainers and had bathed Blackie, before settling down to work out his new computer game. He'd had enough dog-training for one day.

He was just about to tell Mandy about his adventure with the puppy when his mum arrived back and called him downstairs. 'I'll talk to you later,' he said.

Soon afterwards, the phone rang again. Mrs Hunter went to answer it.

'It's for you, James,' she called. She looked puzzled when he came to the phone. 'It's the local TV station,' she said. 'What on earth do they want?'

James soon found out. Ian's dad had phoned them to tell them what had happened. They wanted to interview James and there was to be a story about the rescue on the local news at tea-time. When he put the phone down he explained to his mum what had happened.

'That was very brave of you, James,' she said, shaking her head. 'But it could also have been very dangerous.'

'I know, Mum,' James replied. 'But I was careful.'

Mrs Hunter smiled and gave James a hug. 'I know you were,' she replied. Then she bent to hug Blackie too. 'And you're a very brave dog,' she said. She looked up at James. 'Next time, leave it up to Blackie, OK?'

'I will,' James said with a grin.

And later still there was a frantic knocking at the front door. Mandy stood there, her eyes shining with excitement. She had seen the news report.

'James! Why didn't you tell me about the puppy?'

James shrugged. 'I was going to but—'

To his horror, Mandy threw her arms round him and gave him a hug. 'James, you're a hero!'

When he managed to pull away he said, going red

as usual, 'It wasn't me, it was Blackie. He's the hero.'

Mandy bent down to cuddle Blackie. 'Oh, Blackie, you're so brilliant.' She straightened up. 'There you are,' she said matter-of-factly. 'I knew all our training would pay off in the end. I bet he'll bring back everything we throw for him now.'

But James wasn't so sure. 'I'd wait and see if I were you,' he said with a grin. 'He might be pretty good at retrieving drowning puppies, but sticks are a different thing altogether.'

Blackie barked and stood up on his back legs to lick James's face.

Mandy burst out laughing. 'I've got a feeling he's telling you you're right,' she said.

Read more about Blackie's adventures in Animal Ark Pets, **Puppy Puzzle.**

Manor Farm
Guest House
Bed & Breakfast
Tea Rooms

Donkey dilemma

'Oh, no . . . look, there's Dorian!' Mandy exclaimed. 'He's on the loose again.'

Mandy's dad, Adam Hope, pulled up beside a brown donkey cropping the grass on the side of the road. Mandy and James were accompanying him to Walton Market for the annual horse and pony sale. School was closed for the day for teacher training and Mr Hope had to visit the sale to check that the animals were in good condition. Mandy and James had jumped at the chance to go with him.

As Mr Hope pulled up, the old donkey raised his head and brayed. Mandy and James piled out of the car and ran towards him.

'Dorian, what *are* you doing?' Mandy put her arms around the donkey's neck and gave him a hug.

'He's escaping,' James said, as he ran his hand over the donkey's rough neck.

But Mandy knew this wasn't really true. Dorian was well looked after by Mr and Mrs Nolan and their son Jack, who were the new owners of Manor Farm. He had stayed on at Manor Farm when the previous owners had moved and Dorian's stable companion, Ivanhoe, a magnificent show horse, had been sold. Dorian missed Ivanhoe and it seemed the old donkey thought he might find his friend if he looked hard enough. Unhappily his search was in vain. 'No,' Mandy replied. 'He's lonely.'

By now, Mr Hope had got out of the Land-rover. 'Come on, you two,' he said. 'I've got to get to the market before the sale starts, not halfway through it.'

'We can't leave Dorian here,' Mandy said. 'He could get hurt if he wanders on to the main road. You go on, Dad. We'll take him back.'

Mr Hope reluctantly agreed. He knew Mandy and James loved visiting Walton Market but he wouldn't have time to come back for them. 'If you're sure,' he said. 'And you'd better tell those new people at the farm to keep their gates shut.'

'It was probably one of their visitors,' James said, as

they led Dorian back along the lane towards the farm. The new owners had turned Manor Farm into a bed and breakfast guest house with a tearoom.

'Probably,' Mandy said as they passed the big sign with an arrow pointing to the farm. As they walked up the long drive she could see the white tables and chairs set out on the lawn with bright umbrellas to shelter visitors from the sun. There was a builders' truck parked outside the stable block and the sound of hammering came from inside.

As they went through the gate, Jack came running out. 'Dorian! What are we going to do with you?' Jack's fair hair shone in the sun as he scolded the old donkey gently.

'You really should keep all your gates shut,' James remarked.

Jack had taken hold of Dorian's mane and was leading him towards the paddock where he lived. Part of it had been fenced off into smaller areas. 'I know,' he said. 'One of the builders left it open. I was just going to look for Dorian when you turned up. Thanks for bringing him back.'

Mandy patted Dorian's neck as Jack closed the gate. 'There you are, old boy. Now for goodness sake behave yourself.'

Dorian looked at her with big, sad eyes. Mandy's heart turned over with pity as she patted him again. 'Poor Dorian,' she said softly.

'Dad's a bit fed up with him,' Jack told them. 'He said we've got to get rid of him if we can't control him.'

Mandy's hand flew to her mouth. Get rid of him! Surely Mr Nolan didn't mean he would send Dorian for slaughter. Dorian's previous owner had threatened that once. 'What does he mean?' she asked Jack in horror.

Jack shrugged. 'I'm not sure. And you see, we're having a pets' corner, so no one's going to get time to search for him if he keeps wandering off.'

'What kind of pets are you getting?' James asked.

'Rabbits and guinea-pigs probably,' Jack replied. 'And Dad wants some ducks. Mum's going to ask your mum's advice, Mandy.'

Mandy bit her lip. Rabbits and guinea-pigs were great but they wouldn't be much company for Dorian. He would just go on being lonely for ever . . . unless Jack's dad carried out his threat to get rid of him. She felt tears prick the backs of her eyelids. When Jack and his parents took over responsibility for Dorian she had thought everything would be all right. Now it wasn't turning out to be all right at all.

'A pets' corner will be great, won't it?' James said on the way home. 'They might let us help look after them.'

Mandy was miles away, racking her brains for ideas. They had to find a solution to Dorian's loneliness before it was too late. 'Sorry?' She suddenly realised James had said something.

'I said a pets' corner will be great,' he repeated.

Mandy managed a smile. 'Yes, brilliant. But what about poor old Dorian?'

James gave a sigh. 'I reckon if he doesn't start behaving himself his days are numbered.'

Mandy thought about James's words all day. Dorian didn't deserve that. He'd been a faithful companion to Ivanhoe and had never harmed anyone. His only crime was being lonely and that was something he couldn't help.

Later that day, Mr Hope came in, exhausted from his day at the horse sale. The sale attracted entries from all over the county. Horses, ponies and donkeys, as well as saddlery, were auctioned off to eager bidders.

'There were hundreds of people,' he said as he sat down at the tea table. 'The sale of tack went on for two hours before they even got around to selling the animals.'

Mandy gave a sigh. She would really have loved to have been there, helping her dad examine the animals to make sure they were fit to be sold. But it could sometimes be heartbreaking too ... Not everyone knew how to look after horses and ponies properly and some brought them to the sale looking half-starved and ill. Those were the ones that had to be withdrawn with a stern warning from Mr Hope and the RSPCA inspectors.

Mrs Hope set a pot of tea on the table and sat down. 'It's been a busy day here too.' She reeled off a list of patients. 'How about you, Mandy, what have you been up to?'

'She's been rescuing donkeys,' Mr Hope said with a chuckle. 'Did you get Dorian back to Manor Farm OK?'

Mandy had just finished telling them the story when the phone rang. It was James, asking Mandy if she would like to take Blackie for a walk to Monkton Spinney after tea. As she came back into the kitchen she heard her mum and dad talking.

'Was she in good condition?' Mrs Hope was asking.

'Yes,' Mandy's dad replied. 'It was just that no one wanted her. Shame, she would have made a brilliant family pet.'

'Who would?' Mandy asked, sitting back down at the table.

'A little jenny donkey,' her dad said. 'She was at the sale with her foal. The foal went to a family just the other side of Walton but they didn't want the mother.'

'Poor thing,' Mandy said.

'Yes . . . and the owner didn't want her either. He said he no longer had a use for her now his children had grown up.'

'But what's going to happen to her?' Mandy asked anxiously.

Mr Hope sighed. 'He's taken her back for now but I think she'll have to go to a dealer eventually.'

'A dealer!' Mandy was horrified. Dealers often sold animals for slaughter regardless of their age or condition.

Mrs Hope looked at her daughter. 'Mandy, you know this kind of thing happens all the time.'

'I know,' Mandy replied. 'But a little jenny donkey . . . someone must want her.'

Suddenly a picture of Dorian flashed into her head. She turned to her mum, her eyes shining. 'I know,' she said. 'Dorian . . . he'll want her.'

Mr Hope laughed. 'Yes, but I doubt Mr and Mrs Nolan will. They have a job controlling one donkey, let alone two.'

'Yes, but don't you see?' Mandy cried. 'He wouldn't need controlling if he had a companion. He's just lonely, that's all. When he goes wandering off, it's to look for a friend.'

Mrs Hope smiled gently. 'You don't know that, Mandy. Once an animal gets a wanderlust it's hard to cure it.'

Mandy shook her head. 'No . . . I *know* he's lonely.'

Mr and Mrs Hope exchanged glances.

'Well, Mandy,' her mum said, 'you could tell Mr Nolan about the little jenny, but I don't hold out much hope.'

'Right,' Mandy pushed back her chair. 'I'll ask him now.' There was no time like the present. The jenny donkey was under threat and if they didn't act quickly it might be too late.

But Mr Nolan didn't like the idea at all. 'Sorry,' he said to Mandy when she phoned to ask him. 'That Dorian's bad enough. If the pets' corner takes off and attracts a lot more visitors, the last thing we want is another uncontrollable animal around.'

'But—' Mandy began.

'Sorry,' Mr Nolan said firmly. 'Rabbits and guinea-pigs are more up our street. In fact I'm thinking of getting rid of Dorian anyway. He costs quite a bit to feed and I'm not sure we can really afford him any more.'

'Yes,' Mandy said. 'Jack told us. But surely you wouldn't—' She felt a hand on her arm and turned to see her mum standing there shaking her head.

'OK, Mr Nolan,' she said with a sigh. 'Thanks anyway.' She put the phone down and burst into tears.

Mrs Hope put her arm round her and hugged her close. 'Now don't get upset, Mandy. You can't take all the animal problems of the world under your wing, you know.'

'I know,' she sobbed, 'but poor old Dorian and the poor little jenny donkey . . . it's just not fair!'

'I'm going up to Manor Farm,' Mrs Hope said the following day. 'Do you want to come with me?'

'Dorian's not sick, is he?' Mandy asked anxiously. She had just finished cleaning out the cages in the residential unit at the back of the surgery.

Mrs Hope shook her head. 'No, Mrs Nolan wants to chat about their pets' corner. Apparently the work's nearly finished and they'll be ready to take in some animals next week.'

Mandy was glad of the chance to reassure herself that Dorian was all right. She hadn't been able to get him out of her mind since yesterday; nor the little jenny donkey her dad had told her about.

Dorian's old brown face was looking over the stable door at them when they arrived. Mandy noticed the door had a new bolt.

'He'd learned to open it, so one of the builders fixed a new one,' Jack told Mandy when Mrs Hope had gone inside to talk to Mrs Nolan.

There were several people sitting having tea and scones on the lawn and the car park was full. Just then two small girls detached themselves from a family that had just arrived and came running over to them.

'Can we ride him?' One of the girls stood on tiptoe to pat Dorian's nose. He snuffled gently at her hand.

Jack shook his head. 'We don't give donkey rides,' he said.

The children's mum came to look for them. She grinned when she saw Dorian. 'He's a nice chap.' She rubbed his forelock. 'I had a donkey when I was a child. My brother and I rode him everywhere.'

'Dorian's retired now,' Jack said.

'Pity,' the woman replied. 'I run a summer club for children. I'd have loved to bring them up here for donkey rides.'

Indoors, Jack's mother was preparing cream teas for the visitors while discussing pets with Mrs Hope. Jack told her what the woman had said.

Mrs Nolan looked thoughtful. 'It is a pity,' she said. 'We might have been able to persuade your dad to keep Dorian if he could earn his keep.'

On the way home in the car Mandy sat quietly in the back seat. A plan was forming in her head. Donkey rides . . . it *would* be a great way of earning money. Enough for a donkey's keep – maybe enough for two donkeys . . .

But the problem was, how were they going to persuade Mr Nolan to have another donkey when he didn't particularly want the one he'd already got?

'Dad,' Mandy said later when she had worked out her scheme, 'will you do me a favour?'

Mr Hope looked dubious when she told him her plan. 'Mandy, I'm not sure.'

'Please, Dad,' she begged. 'There's no harm in asking.'

That was one of her gran's favourite sayings. And Gran was right. There never *was* any harm in asking.

A couple of hours later, Jack Nolan came running out as a Land-rover and trailer drew up outside Manor Farm. Mr Hope and Mandy got out. They went round to the back and opened the tailgate. Mandy went in and minutes later emerged leading a small, honey-coloured jenny donkey wearing a saddle and red bridle. Mr Hope's call to the auctioneers to obtain her owner's phone number had been just in time to save her going to a dealer.

'Oh . . . she's gorgeous.' Jack fondled the donkey's velvet nose. Several people having sandwiches and tea on the lawn got up from their chairs and came to pet the new arrival.

They weren't the only ones who were interested. In the paddock, Dorian lifted his head from the grass. His ears were pricked and his nostrils flared into the breeze. Suddenly he gave a loud bray, kicked up his heels and came galloping to the fence. The jenny donkey looked at him and brayed back, a soft bray, as she looked at him with big melting brown eyes.

'Excuse me, please . . .' Mandy led Jenny – the name suited her perfectly – carefully through the crowd of people and went towards Dorian. He brayed again, leaning his stubby neck as far across the fence as he was able. Jenny lifted her nose to his and blew softly into his nostrils.

Mandy didn't know how she stopped the tears that threatened to run down her cheeks. Dorian and Jenny were friends already.

Now all they had to do was persuade Mr Nolan that Jenny would not only be a great companion for Dorian

but she would earn both their keeps by giving rides to children who visited Manor Farm. And what was more, Jenny's owner had said the Nolans could have her free of charge, so she wouldn't cost them a thing to buy.

Mrs Nolan was already there, patting and stroking Jenny as if she had known her all her life. She looked at Mr Hope. 'She's lovely . . . so gentle. I'm sure she'll be a great hit with the children. I'm just not sure what my husband will say.'

'Well, here's Dad now,' Jack said as a saloon car came through the gate and up the drive. 'So you're about to find out.'

At first, Mr Nolan had a face like thunder. But his anger soon began to melt as Jenny nuzzled his arm and charmed him with her soft brown gaze.

And when she'd given rides to several children and had behaved perfectly, he melted some more.

He was finally won over when they unsaddled Jenny and turned her out with Dorian. Mr Nolan smiled as the two donkeys raced round the paddock, kicking up their heels with sheer happiness. It was obvious the jenny donkey had won his heart too.

Jenny had brought new life to Dorian and a chance for him to enjoy his old age in peace. Mandy knew the two creatures were going to be great companions

– Dorian would never need to go wandering off again!

The two donkeys finally settled down and came back to the fence. Mr Nolan patted Dorian's neck. 'Good old boy,' he murmured. Even *he* had been moved by the sight of the two donkeys so full of joy.

Dorian was nuzzling one of Mandy's sleeves, Jenny the other. 'I hope you two will be very happy,' she said, laughing.

And Dorian gave a loud bray that Mandy was absolutely sure meant *Yes, thank you, I'm sure we will*.

*Read more about Dorian's adventures in **Donkey on the Doorstep***.

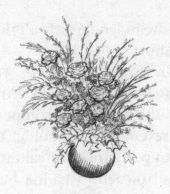

Amber takes the prize

'That looks just like one of Mrs Ponsonby's hats,' said Alex Hastings, looking at her mother's flower arrangement.

Mrs Hastings laughed at her five-year-old daughter's serious expression and ruffled the little girl's curly red hair. Alex was sitting at the kitchen table with Amber, her black, brown and white kitten in her lap.

'Don't say that at the Welford Show,' Mrs Hastings said. 'Mrs Ponsonby is very proud of her hats. She might not like them compared to a flower arrangement.'

Mrs Ponsonby was the bossiest woman in Welford.

She made sure she judged nearly all the events at the annual village show.

'Mrs Ponsonby's hats are *terrible*,' William, Alex's brother, said. He looked at Amber. 'Are you going to enter Amber in the best kitten competition, Alex?'

William was seven, two years older than Alex.

Alex's face lit up. 'Can I?' she said to her mum.

Mrs Hastings frowned. 'I hadn't heard about the kitten competition,' she said. 'But if there is one you should certainly enter Amber. I'm sure she has a chance of winning. You keep her so nicely.'

Alex gave Amber a cuddle. 'She's the best kitten in the world,' she said.

'There,' said Mrs Hastings, tucking a purple dahlia into the front of her flower arrangement. 'That's the best I can do.'

'It looks lovely,' said Alex.

'Hmm,' said Mrs Hastings. 'Let's just hope it doesn't wilt before the competition this afternoon.'

'I could give it a spray with my water pistol,' William said helpfully. 'That'll keep it fresh.'

'No, thank you, William,' Mrs Hastings said firmly. 'I know the damage you can do with your water pistol. Now, let's have lunch and then it'll be time to go to the show.'

William grinned. He was looking forward to the show too.

'I've been practising for the coconut shy,' he said.

Mr Hastings came into the kitchen just as he finished speaking.

'And I've been replacing a pane of glass in the garden shed window,' he said. 'So much for your practising.'

'Oops,' said William, and Alex grinned. William was a rotten shot – only he wouldn't admit it.

'It looks great,' said William, staring around the field. There were tents dotted here and there and trestle tables crammed with homemade baking. Stalls were set up under awnings around the edge of the field – hoopla, wet sponge throwing and, of course, the coconut shy. Behind the coconut shy was an open-fronted tent with a banner above it. It said 'PET COMPETITIONS' in big letters. Beside it was the floral art table with a blue and white striped awning above it.

'Do I take Amber over there?' asked Alex, pointing to the notice.

'There's Mandy Hope and James Hunter,' Mrs Hastings said, balancing her flower arrangement on her arm. 'They'll be able to tell you what to do. I'd better get these flowers over to the floral art table before I drop them.'

'And I'm going to queue up for the coconut

shy,' said William, sprinting off.

Alex waved to Mandy. She and James had rescued Amber when she was lost in the snow at Christmas. They always enjoyed seeing her. Now they walked over to see Alex and the little kitten.

'Doesn't she look lovely,' Mandy said as she reached out a hand and tickled Amber under the chin.

Alex nodded. 'I'm going to put her in for the best kitten competition,' Alex said.

'You'd better hurry then,' said James. 'Mrs Ponsonby has just announced it. Everybody has to bring their kittens into the tent now.'

'But you'll have to get her dressed up first,' Mandy said.

'Dressed up?' said Alex, puzzled.

Mandy nodded. 'It's a competition for the best-dressed kitten,' she said.

Alex's face fell. 'I thought it was for the best *kept* kitten,' she said. 'Does that mean I can't enter her?'

Mandy looked doubtful. 'I don't see how you can,' she said. 'Look!'

Alex looked to where Mandy was pointing. A row of children were lining up outside the tent. Every one of them carried a kitten – and every kitten was wearing something special. There was one with a little red hat with bells on, another had a bright yellow waistcoat and several had bows round their necks.

'There's Richard Tanner,' said James. 'What's he doing here?'

A dark-haired boy of about eleven turned and waved to them. He towered above all the little kids in the row. None of the others looked more than six years old.

'He must be entering Duchess,' Mandy said, moving towards the tent. 'Let's go and ask him.'

Richard's cat, Duchess, had a ruff round her neck and four white socks on her paws. Duchess didn't look as if she liked being dressed up. She kept trying to drag the socks off with her teeth but she couldn't reach them properly because of the ruff. Richard didn't look too happy either.

'Hi, Richard,' said Mandy. 'I didn't know you were entering Duchess for this.'

Richard turned a bit red. 'Just don't tell anybody,' he muttered. 'Mum made me do it. She thought it would be a good idea. She even made this ruff. Duchess hates it.'

'I don't blame her,' said James. 'It's not exactly Duchess's style, is it?'

Duchess was well known in Welford as a seriously dignified cat.

'What if I win?' Richard said comically. 'I'd probably get my picture in the local paper. I'd never live it down.'

Mandy giggled. 'Poor Richard,' she said. 'And poor Duchess. She hates that ruff. The other cats don't seem to mind though.'

'They're kittens,' said Richard. 'They don't know any better.'

'Why don't you just slope off?' suggested James.

Richard looked around furtively. 'Mum's at the floral art stall,' he said. 'She's watching me.'

They looked across at the next stall and Mrs Tanner beamed back at them. She gave Richard a wave and a thumbs-up sign. Richard groaned.

'Amber would love to get dressed up,' said Alex stoutly. 'I often dress her up in doll's clothes.'

'Yeugh!' said Richard. 'You and my mum would get on just fine, Alex.'

'Disqualified,' boomed a voice behind them.

Alex looked up. Mrs Ponsonby was standing over them, glaring at Duchess.

'Your hat looks just like my mum's flower arrangement,' said Alex, and Mrs Ponsonby turned the glare on her.

'*What* was that?' she said.

'Alex's mum did that flower arrangement,' Mandy said quickly, pointing to the next-door tent where a row of floral art decorations was set out.

'Hmmph,' said Mrs Ponsonby. 'Children today mumble all the time,' she said. 'Sometimes I can't understand a word they say.'

'Just as well,' said James under his breath and Mrs Ponsonby looked suspiciously at him.

'Did you say Duchess was disqualified, Mrs Ponsonby?' Richard asked hopefully.

'I certainly did,' said Mrs Ponsonby firmly. 'And I don't want any arguments, Richard. Duchess is a cat, not a kitten. And this is a kitten competition.'

Richard tried to look disappointed. 'Oh, well,' he said. 'That's the way it goes, I suppose.'

Mrs Ponsonby looked even more suspicious as Richard turned away. She had clearly expected an argument – and she looked a bit put out not to get one!

'Duchess is disqualified because she's a cat not a kitten, Mum,' Richard said as they passed the floral art stall.

'Are you sure you're not just saying that to get out of it?' Mrs Tanner said, putting the finishing touches to the floral ring she was exhibiting. It was a little posy ring, about the size of a small plate, made up of tiny pink rosebuds and ferns.

'Mrs Ponsonby said so,' Alex replied. 'And I can't enter Amber because she isn't dressed up.'

Mrs Hastings looked up from her flower arrangement. 'Oh, Alex, what a pity,' she said.

'Do you want to enter her?' asked Richard.

Alex nodded vehemently. 'More than anything in the world,' she said.

'That's no problem then,' said Richard, taking off Duchess's socks. 'Take this stuff. I don't need it any more.'

Alex's face lit up. 'Can I?' she said. 'Really?'

Mrs Tanner smiled. 'Why not?' she said. 'At least that way my efforts won't have been wasted.'

Alex held Amber up and looked into the kitten's golden eyes. 'You're going to get dressed up, Amber,' she said. 'I bet you'll win.'

'You'd better hurry,' said Mandy, looking round at the table outside the pet competition tent. 'Mrs Ponsonby is getting the kittens lined up for judging.'

Richard undid the ruff from around Duchess's neck and Alex held Amber up to him. The little kitten struggled slightly as Richard put his hand out to take her.

Just then there was a shout from the coconut shy behind them.

'It's my turn now,' William yelled. 'Watch me!'

Alex turned, fumbling her grip on Amber. The kitten leaped for the floral art table just as William's ball came hurtling through the air – and landed on the sloping awning over the table.

'William!' Mrs Hastings shouted.

'Oops! Missed again,' said William.

'Watch out!' said Mandy.

They all looked up. The ball began to roll down the blue and white striped awning, gathering speed as it went. It rolled over the edge, bounced once on the ground – and landed right in the middle of the floral art table, startling Amber.

'Grab her!' James yelled.

Too late. The little kitten took off at speed, diving in among the flower displays and heading off down the length of the table.

'My floral ring!' shouted Mrs Tanner as Amber shot off.

'Amber!' cried Alex, rushing after her kitten.

Mandy, James and Richard raced after her, closely followed by Mrs Tanner and Mrs Hastings. Amber had dived into the posy ring and now it was firmly settled round the kitten's neck – like a rosebud ruff!

'Catch her!' Richard said, making a dive for the kitten.

Amber had stopped at the end of the table, hesitating to jump all the way down to the ground.

Richard reached out but Amber took fright and leaped again – not to the ground but between the floral art table and the next one, the one where the kittens were lined up waiting to be judged.

Mrs Ponsonby turned to the kitten as it landed on the table, then looked at the rest as they ran up breathless and panting.

'Well, well,' she said. 'I must say that's cutting it a bit fine. You were very nearly too late with your entry, Alex, but as it is I'll overlook it.'

Alex opened her mouth to speak but Mandy put her fingers to her lips. 'Wait,' she said. 'Mrs Ponsonby thinks you've entered Amber for the competition.'

'But she isn't dressed up,' said Alex.

Mandy giggled. 'Yes she is,' she said. 'Look at her!'

Alex looked at Amber. As well as the floral ring around her neck, Amber had collected a few bits of bunting and several sticky bows on her way across the floral art table.

'She's about as dressed up as you can get,' said James.

Mrs Ponsonby looked fondly at Amber. 'I must say,'

she said. 'All the kittens look lovely but I think this little one takes the prize.' She patted her hat. 'That floral ring reminds me of something. I can't think what.'

William appeared at Alex's side, the ball from the coconut shy in his hand. 'Your hat!' he said to Mrs Ponsonby.

Mrs Hastings looked at him. 'William!' she said dangerously. 'I want a word with you.'

'I was trying to hit the coconuts,' William said.

'And, after all, if it hadn't been for William, Amber wouldn't have won the prize,' said Mandy.

'What about your floral ring, Mum?' Richard said.

Mrs Tanner grinned. 'I'd say that's won one prize already,' she said. 'And if I freshen it up it might win another.'

'Go on, Alex,' said Mrs Hastings. 'Go and get Amber's prize.'

Mrs Ponsonby was standing with a huge rosette in her hand, looking puzzled. 'Your kitten is so well dressed I can't find anywhere to put it,' she said.

Alex marched up to the table. 'That's all right, Mrs Ponsonby,' she said. 'You can put it on me.'

'So I can,' said Mrs Ponsonby, smiling – and she pinned the rosette on Alex's jumper!

*Read more about Amber's adventures in **Kitten in the Cold**.*

Bunny Trouble

'*Dip, dip, dip, my blue ship, sails on the water, like a cup and saucer, O-U-T spells out!*' Imogen Parker Smythe chanted the rhyme over the heads of five baby rabbits. Her chubby finger pointed at one of the fluffy brown balls of fur.

Mandy frowned at James. This didn't seem like the best way to decide who should keep which of the seven-week-old rabbit kittens.

'Immi darling, perhaps it would be better to let John decide which of Button's babies he wants to keep, since you chose the names of the little bunny rabbits.' Imogen's mother hovered in the background. 'Or at least take it in turns!'

Five babies. Two each for John Hardy and Imogen Parker Smythe. One left over. Mandy held her breath.

'Oh!' Imogen screwed up her round face. The corners of her mouth went down. 'But *I* want to choose!'

'It's OK. I don't mind which ones I have!' John spoke up, polite as ever.

Mandy smiled at him. 'If I was him, I'd want to throttle Imogen!' she whispered to James.

'Plee-eease!' the selfish seven-year-old rolled her eyes at her mother. 'Button and Barney were my rabbits in the first place; before I shared them with John!'

'That's true,' James whispered back to Mandy. Imogen's parents had thrown a party in the garden and Mandy, James and John had been invited along with their parents. The other guests had gone home now, but the children had stayed on to decide the future of Button and Barney's offspring.

Mandy nodded. If only Imogen weren't so spoiled.

'But, darling . . . !'

'Plee-ease!'

'Let Imogen choose,' John insisted. He'd been away at school when the babies were born and the Parker Smythes had been looking after them all at Beacon House. It was only now that he was home for the summer and ready to take his turn at looking after

Button and Barney that the rabbit family would have
to be split up.

'Very well.' Mrs Parker Smythe gave in.

Imogen clapped her hands and startled the rabbits.
They hopped up and down the run on the smooth
green lawn outside the big manor house on the hill
above Welford.

'Brandy, Benny, Babs and Betty!' The little girl went
down on her hands and knees and crawled after them,
poking her face against the wire mesh. 'And Bubble!'
She pointed to the smallest rabbit of all; a soft, round
ball of pale fawn fur sitting quietly in a corner.

'Choose two,' her mum insisted.

'I want a girl and a boy!'

'A doe and a buck,' James chipped in helpfully.

'A girl and a boy rabbit!' Imogen ignored him and
lifted the trapdoor on the roof of the run. She scooped
out the nearest baby. 'I'll have you, Babs!' A second
scoop with her podgy arm. 'And you, Benny!'

The little rabbits wriggled and kicked. From inside
the nearby hutch, Button watched anxiously.

'That leaves Brandy and Betty for you,' Mandy
murmured to John.

He gazed at the two babies left hopping and bobbing
on the grass. Their long ears flicked, their button-
noses twitched and their silky coats gleamed. 'That's
fine by me!' he smiled. He turned to the fifth baby

rabbit tucked away in the corner of the run.

'. . . And Bubble!' Imogen announced, thrusting Benny and Babs into her mother's arms and making a dive for the run. 'Bubble stays here with me too!'

Mandy saw John's eyes flicker shut. He was a small, neat boy with dark, wavy hair. He was never untidy, never noisy or rude. But he was mad about rabbits. He stepped in front of Imogen and stood in her way.

'I'd like to take Bubble home with me, if you don't mind,' he said quietly.

'That's not fair!' Imogen sprang back at him. Her pigtails flew out as she spun round to face her mother. 'I want Bubble! Bubble's mine!'

'I would look after him better,' John insisted. 'He's the smallest. He needs special care.'

'Mu-ummy!' Imogen wailed.

It was stalemate. Mrs Parker Smythe ran a hand through her blonde hair and looked helplessly across the lawn at the big house.

'What will they do now, chop Bubble in half?' James muttered.

Mandy frowned. John was polite, but he was stubborn. And he was right about the smallest kitten needing special care. Bubble had always been the frail one; he had been the last one to be born, the lightest, and the most timid.

As Imogen whined and John refused to give way,

Mrs Parker Smythe washed her hands of the problem. 'Let's not have a scene, Immikins dear.'

'Not fair!' Imogen muttered. She glowered at John. He stared back, arms folded, mouth set firm.

'Let's ask Daddy,' the diplomatic mother decided. 'What do you say, darling? Let's go inside and let *him* decide!'

Mandy had seen Button's babies being born. The Parker Smythes had brought the pregnant mother into Animal Ark and asked for a vet to be present at the births.

'It's not really necessary,' Adam Hope had told them. 'The births will happen very quickly and easily. Button can cope by herself, believe me.'

'Better to be safe than sorry,' Mrs Parker Smythe had insisted.

The five babies had been born without fur. Their eyes and ears were closed; they were completely helpless.

'Aren't they beautiful?' Mandy had placed them where the mother could lick them clean. Soon they were all suckling strongly.

Imogen had named them on the spot: Brandy, Benny, Babs, Betty and Bubble.

After one week, their fur had begun to grow. At two weeks their eyes had opened. Now, seven weeks after the birth, they were almost weaned and ready to leave their mother.

'Imogen and John are arguing over who keeps Bubble,' Mandy told her mum and dad at breakfast on the day after the garden party.

She and James had left Beacon House with John. All the way down the hill into the village, he'd repeated the reasons why he should keep the fifth baby rabbit.

'What does Imogen Parker-Smythe know about rabbits in any case? She just thinks of them as fluffy toys!'

'I think she does care, deep down.' Mandy had tried to be kind.

John had snorted. He strode off to the pub where he lived with a parting shot. 'She doesn't know the first thing about them. She doesn't even think they're real animals!'

'Sounds like trouble,' Adam Hope said now from behind his newspaper. 'Bunny trouble.'

'You say it's the smallest rabbit they're arguing over?' Emily Hope had only been half-listening to Mandy's account. She was due to drive the Land-rover out on her morning calls. But she paused at the door with some startling news. 'Well, if it's Bubble you're talking about, the situation's changed.'

'How come?' Mandy stopped chewing her toast.

'Mrs Parker Smythe rang me late last night.'

'What about?' Alarm bells rang in Mandy's head.

'About Bubble. Apparently Imogen's very upset. She went to feed the rabbits last thing before she went to bed, and guess what: Bubble was missing.'

'Missing?' Mandy stared.

Mrs Hope nodded. 'Vanished. Nowhere to be found.'

'End of story,' Adam Hope said quietly. 'No rabbit: no argument. Full-stop.'

'It's all John Hardy's fault!' Imogen's tear-stained face peered at James and Mandy through the iron gates of Beacon House. 'He stole Bubble from me!'

James shook his head. 'He wouldn't do that!'

'He did! He crept back here after everyone had gone home. I left all five babies in the rabbit run with Button and Barney while I went inside. When I came back, Bubble was gone!' Imogen's bottom lip quivered as she told them what had happened.

'But you didn't actually see John steal him?' Like James, Mandy couldn't believe it.

'I didn't have to. I just know it was him!' Fresh tears welled in Imogen's eyes.

'And you're sure Bubble was stolen? He didn't just escape?' Mandy asked. She scanned the grounds of the Parker Smythe house with its laurel bushes and tall beech trees.

The tears spilled over. 'We looked everywhere. John stole him. I *know* he did!'

'. . . Missing?' The shock registered in John Hardy's dark brown eyes. 'Bubble? He can't be!'

'Imogen thinks you took him,' Mandy explained. She and James had come straight down from Beacon House.

'Me?'

James nodded and sighed. 'She thinks you crept back and stole him.'

John stared blankly back.

'Did you?' Mandy asked outright.

He laughed scornfully. 'Oh, sure! I would do that, wouldn't I?' He turned to go inside the pub and slam the door.

'But did you?' she persisted, putting her hand out to stop him. She had to be sure.

John's eyes narrowed. 'Believe Imogen, why don't you?'

'We're not saying we believe her,' James put in. 'We just need to know.'

But John wouldn't listen. He leaned heavily on the door, pushing them off the step into the yard. 'I don't care. Think what you like!' he snapped.

The door slammed shut in their faces.

'Come in, come in!' Mrs Parker Smythe invited them inside the house.

By mid-morning, Mandy and James had been up and down Beacon Hill like yo-yos, trying to solve the mystery of the missing baby rabbit. They had Imogen's version and John's angry response. Now it was time to take a look for themselves.

'Imogen's too upset to talk to anyone,' her mother explained in a whisper. She glanced across to the swimming-pool room. 'She's having a quiet swim. But I'm sure she'll be very grateful for your help. You say you'd like to search the garden?'

Mandy nodded. 'I know Bubble's been missing since last night, and he could be anywhere by now, but we'd still like to take a look.'

So Mrs Parker Smythe led them out to the rabbit run, where the four remaining youngsters groomed themselves and played under Button's watchful eye.

James crouched and examined the wire mesh. 'No sign of a break-out,' he reported. The mesh was firmly nailed to the wooden frame all the way along the run.

'Hmm. I'm not so sure.' Mandy looked again at the corner where Bubble had been sitting the day before. 'Look here.'

She pointed to a clump of dock leaves growing up

and through the holes in the wire mesh. The broad green leaves hid a tiny gap; just big enough for a skinny baby rabbit to squeeze through.

'I bet the Parker Smythes don't know about that!' James breathed. 'And neither do any of the other babies, thank heavens!' He pulled the mesh back into position.

'So much for Imogen's theory!' Mandy thought rapidly. 'If Bubble did break out, where would he make for?'

'Somewhere where there's food! Food!' James suggested. 'Food like oats, carrots, apples, hay . . . !'

'Salad, milk, cream.' Mandy figured it out. 'Listen, James, there was loads of food around yesterday, left over from the party!'

'Sandwiches, cakes, chocolate biscuits!' James followed Mandy up the sloping lawn. The food for the garden party had been set out in front of the open pool-room doors. A hungry little rabbit escaping from his run would have had no problem tracking down the smell.

'And once he'd found the feast and tucked in, what would he do then?' As they drew near the pool, Mandy could hear the splish-splash of Imogen in the deep end through the open doors.

'Find somewhere nice and warm to sleep,' James predicted.

'A dark place, where no one would disturb him.' Mandy stopped under a beech tree, studying the garden tables where the party food had been laid out.

'Somewhere safe,' James agreed. He saw the boxes on the table at the same time as Mandy. Together they broke into a run.

'Hey, what are you doing?' Imogen spotted them through the open glass doors. She puffed and spluttered with surprise.

'Looking for Bubble!' Mandy held a finger to her lips. If the baby rabbit had taken refuge inside one of these cardboard boxes, they mustn't scare him off.

'Not you, Mandy. I meant John Hardy!' Imogen was clambering out of the pool in her bright orange swimming-costume, dripping water everywhere.

Mandy and James spun round to see John hiding behind one of the tall trees by the pool. He stepped out. 'Great minds think alike,' he muttered.

'You mean, you decided to come looking for Bubble too?' James went to meet him while Mandy began to lift the lid of the first box.

John nodded, ignoring Imogen's hostile stare. 'It stands to reason. I know I didn't steal him. So *she* must have let the poor thing escape. He's lost in this huge garden.'

'Escape . . . lost?' Imogen echoed.

'Shh!' Mandy warned. The box was full of plates

and glasses. She moved on to the next. 'This one's been left open!'

She peered inside. The box held some of the leftover party food. There were crisps in plastic bags, cakes in containers. And Bubble!

The frightened rabbit peered up at her with big, round eyes. He twitched his nose, turned and tried to hide in a corner. But his long ears stuck up from behind the cake box, and the tip of his white tail poked out of the side.

'There!' Mandy cooed as she slipped her fingers under his soft tummy and picked him up. 'No one's going to harm you. We're just very glad to see you, that's all!'

'I'm sorry!' Imogen stood shamefaced by the side of the rabbit run after James had shown her the hole where Bubble had escaped. 'I shouldn't have blamed you, John.'

'That's OK.' He accepted her apology. 'I suppose all this only happened because we both like rabbits so much.'

Imogen swallowed hard. 'You can have Bubble if you really want!'

'No, it's OK. You keep him!' John said grudgingly through gritted teeth.

James stood open-mouthed.

'Hang on!' Mandy looked at Bubble worriedly. He

was trembling after his big adventure, and his nose was wet and runny. 'I think he's poorly. If he doesn't see a vet straight away, *no one's* going to be looking after him!'

Gently Mandy stroked the little rabbit and suggested to Mrs Parker Smythe that they send for her mum. Bubble nestled in her arms, his head tucked under Mandy's chin, his ears and whiskers tickling her neck.

'What's wrong with him?' Imogen whispered.

'I'm not sure. But we definitely ought to have him looked at.' When rabbits got sick, they often faded fast, she knew.

'Don't worry, perhaps we're all worrying over nothing.' Mrs Parker Smythe came back from making the phone call. 'And Mrs Hope will be here in a few minutes.'

A few minutes for them all to worry; Bubble sat and shivered in Mandy's arms, looking dully at his brothers and sisters playing in the run.

Then Mandy's mum arrived with her big vet's bag. She took the tiny patient's temperature and shone a light in his eyes. She looked in his ears and down his throat.

'Well?' Mandy murmured, as the others huddled round. 'How is he?'

Emily Hope smiled. 'Nothing serious,' she told them.

There was one big sigh of relief.

'I'd say this rabbit is suffering from a bad case of over-indulgence, that's all!' Mandy's mum winked at her.

'What's that mean?' Imogen asked.

'That Bubble's eaten too much!' Mandy explained. 'The party food he found in the box was too rich for him.'

'Uh-hum!' Mrs Hope cleared her throat. 'There's just one other thing . . .'

'What's that?' James, Mandy, John and Imogen cried out together.

'Bubble isn't a "he". She's a "she"!'

'A girl rabbit!' Imogen gasped.

'And Babs isn't a "she". He's a "he". So is Betty.' Mrs Hope gave a full report on the other babies. 'I know it was young Imogen who gave them their names in the first place, but I did warn you at the time that it was much too early to tell the girls from the boys! Now, I'm afraid you're going to have to have a major re-think!'

'*Four* boys and a girl!' Imogen blushed to the roots of her hair.

'Never mind, darling. You weren't to know.' Mrs Parker Smythe hid her smiles. 'You could change Babs's name to Bob, and Betty could be Bertie from

now on. How about that?'

Imogen quietly agreed. 'So Benny and Bob belong to me.'

'And Brandy and Bertie are mine,' John confirmed.

'That still leaves Bubble, the tug-of-love bunny,' Mandy reminded them.

'Ah-ha!' It was Emily Hope's turn to speak up again. 'A doe must be kept separate from the bucks, remember. Otherwise you'll have lots more babies on your hands.'

'Oh no!' Mrs Parker Smythe backed off at the very idea. 'I can't go through all this again!'

'Exactly.' Mrs Hope turned to Mandy. 'Any suggestions?'

Mandy still held cute little Bubble firmly in her arms. 'It so happens . . .' she began, looking at James.

'Pets' Parlour!' he went on, nodding and smiling.

'The pet shop in Walton,' Mandy explained.

'We were in there last week,' James said.

'And we heard someone trying to buy a pet rabbit.'

'But there weren't any in the shop.'

'So the girl put her name on a waiting list,' Mandy said quickly. 'Apparently there are lots of people who want them. Geoff, the pet-shop owner, says he knows at least six families who could give a rabbit a good home!'

As she finished speaking, John and Imogen felt all eyes turned on them.

'Well?' Emily Hope prompted.

Imogen looked at John. John looked at Imogen. Mandy and James held their breath. Bubble shuffled and snuggled deeper into Mandy's arms.

'Great idea!' Imogen and John agreed for the very first time. 'Let's take Bubble down there right away!'

Read more about Button and Barney's adventures in **Bunnies in the Bathroom.**

Mrs Ponsonby's Ghost

'A ghost,' Mrs Ponsonby said in a low voice. 'I'm sure there's a ghost haunting Bleakfell Hall.'

Mrs Ponsonby had looked very agitated about something as she'd opened the door to Mandy and James's ring on the bell. They were delivering some pills for Mrs Ponsonby's dog, Pandora.

Mandy had seen at once that something was wrong. Mrs Ponsonby was still wearing her nightdress and the cardigan she had thrown over the top was buttoned up the wrong way. *And* she was wearing a pair of velvet carpet slippers instead of the smart shoes she usually wore, even indoors. Her hair was all over the place. In fact, she looked terrible.

Earlier that morning Mandy had been reading an article about threatened wildlife in her animal magazine when Mr Hope had asked her to deliver Pandora's medication. Mandy wasn't too keen on bossy Mrs Ponsonby but she loved her dogs, Pandora the Pekinese and Toby the mongrel, and welcomed the chance to visit them. She had quickly phoned James and they had set off for Bleakfell Hall on their bikes.

'A ghost!' James's eyes were wide behind his glasses. 'How brilliant!' He had been reading a book about ghosts and was really interested in that kind of thing.

Mandy wasn't so sure. 'What makes you think that?' she asked uneasily.

Mrs Ponsonby took the bottle of pills from Mandy then drew them into the great entrance hall. Mandy had always thought Bleakfell was creepy and all this talk of ghosts seemed to confirm it.

'Noises.' Mrs Ponsonby raised her eyes to the ceiling. 'Up there. Darling Pandora and Toby have been barking almost non-stop. I haven't had any sleep for three nights.'

By now, Toby had come hurtling along the corridor from the kitchen. He threw himself at Mandy and James, trying to reach their faces so he could lick them. Pandora came waddling behind, her tail waving like a banner.

Mandy gave Toby a hug, then bent to stroke Pandora.

James had wandered off, no doubt looking for Mrs Ponsonby's ghost. He had always thought Bleakfell Hall was spooky too. He stood looking at a large portrait of a man in a scarlet cloak with a white ermine collar.

Mrs Ponsonby sat down heavily on one of the huge sofas on either side of the hall, and passed her hand across her forehead. 'If it goes on much longer I'll have to sell up and leave.'

'Oh, Mrs Ponsonby!' Mandy thought that was a bit drastic. 'You can't do that.' She couldn't imagine Welford without Mrs Ponsonby and Pandora and Toby.

'I can't think of another solution,' Mrs Ponsonby said. She suddenly noticed James staring at the portrait. 'I think it might be him,' she said in a low voice, as if the man might hear what she was saying. 'My great-great uncle. Maybe I've done something to offend him.'

Mandy went to stand beside James. The man in the picture looked pretty good-natured to her. Not at all the sort of person to haunt somewhere and frighten people and dogs out of their wits.

'Have you actually seen him, then?' Mandy asked. She gave a little shiver. All this talk of ghosts and noises in the night was giving her the creeps.

'I don't *see* him,' Mrs Ponsonby said. 'I just hear him. *Swish, swish* . . . he was a judge, you know, and wore a long robe. I think that's what's making the noise.'

James had left the portrait and was standing at the bottom of the curving staircase. He stared upwards. 'Where do the noises come from?'

Mrs Ponsonby rose. 'I'll show you.'

Mandy felt quite scared as they climbed the massive staircase, round and round to where the treads narrowed into a spiral that took them to the third floor. Up here, their footsteps echoed on the bare boards and Toby's claws made a scrabbling sound as he ran on ahead of them. His ears were pricked as if he could hear something they couldn't.

'These used to be the servants' bedrooms,' Mrs Ponsonby panted as they reached the top. She threw open one of the doors.

James entered, with Mandy following cautiously. The tiny room had sloping ceilings; there was a hatchway that led up into the roof. A little window looked out over the front drive and the sweeping distant moorland.

James went to the window. 'Great view,' he said. Then he cocked his head to one side. 'I can't hear anything.'

'You should be here at night.' Mrs Ponsonby lowered her voice. 'Pandora and Toby have been rushing up here and won't come down until I tempt them with one of their favourite chocolate biscuits.' She looked over her shoulder as if she was afraid someone might be listening . . . or watching. 'That's when I hear the swishing noise,' she whispered. 'It scares me to death.'

'Why don't you keep the door closed?' Mandy asked.

Mrs Ponsonby shook her head. 'My darlings go completely berserk if I do,' she said.

But James wasn't worried about the dogs going berserk. He was looking at Mrs Ponsonby, his eyes shining with excitement. 'Could we?' he said.

'Could you what?' Mrs Ponsonby looked confused.

'Stay here for a night and listen for the ghost?'

'James!' Mandy said. She wasn't at all sure that's what she wanted to do. And, anyway, Mrs Ponsonby was extremely fussy about who stayed in her house. She felt sure Mrs Ponsonby would never agree.

But to Mandy's surprise, Mrs Ponsonby jumped at the idea.

'Oh, would you, James?' she said. She had picked up the panting Pandora and was cuddling her like a teddy bear. 'And you, Mandy?' Pandora huffed and puffed and wriggled to get down. 'At least if you hear them too then you'll know that my darling dogs and I aren't going completely mad.'

Mandy looked dubious. 'We'll have to check with our parents,' she said. 'They might not let us.'

* * *

'I reckon you're *mad*,' Mandy said to James as they pedalled back towards the village. '*You* might want to go ghost-hunting but I'm not sure I do.'

'Oh, come on,' James encouraged her. 'It'll be great.'

Mandy sighed. James always went along with her schemes, so she supposed that this time she'd better go along with his.

'You want to do *what*?' Mrs Hope exclaimed later, when Mandy asked her if it would be all right.

She laughed when Mandy explained. 'It's really James who wants to,' Mandy said. 'But I said I'd go too if you'd let me.'

Mrs Hope laughed again. 'I can't see why not,' she said. 'There's sure to be a rational explanation. And it'll help Mrs Ponsonby if you find out what it is.'

'James will be upset if it isn't ghosts,' Mandy said, laughing too. She'd managed to see the funny side of it when Mrs Hope explained that old houses often made noises and it was probably a loose tile on the roof, or the wind rushing round one of the chimneys . . . or something.

'Yes, well, by the sound of it Mrs Ponsonby will be glad to solve the mystery,' her mum said.

James arrived ten minutes later armed with sleeping bag, notebook and tape recorder. And his dog, Blackie.

'He's got brilliant hearing,' James said. 'And a brilliant nose. He might even sniff out the ghost for us.'

'And what's *that* for?' Mandy eyed the recorder curiously.

'To tape the noises, of course,' James answered. 'And the notebook's to write down times and places of sightings.'

'James, I'm not sure . . .' Mandy began.

'Mandy, it'll be great,' James insisted. 'It really will.'

Mrs Hope was just going out on a call. She put her head around the kitchen door. 'I'm just going up to Baildon Farm to see a cow with a foot infection. I could drop you off at Bleakfell Hall if you like.'

'Oh, yes please,' James replied.

'Did Mrs Ponsonby say it would be OK to take Blackie?' Mrs Hope asked, before they set off in the Land-rover.

'No, but I'm sure she won't mind,' James said. 'He won't cause any trouble.'

'He *always* causes trouble,' Mandy said, kissing Blackie's velvety nose. 'He's famous for it, aren't you Blackie?'

Blackie licked her cheek.

'Well,' said Mrs Hope, 'just don't be a nuisance . . . any of you.'

* * *

Twilight at Bleakfell Hall was the spookiest time of day. The towers and turrets were shrouded in gloom and owls called to one another across the huge tree-shadowed garden.

Mandy and James had settled themselves in their sleeping bags in the tiny attic room. Blackie had tried to get into James's sleeping bag with him but had finally decided there wasn't enough room and had settled himself on the floor under the window. There weren't any light bulbs so they had brought torches and a box full of sandwiches and crisps in case they got peckish. Mrs Ponsonby had provided them with pillows.

'Not that you'll be able to sleep,' she had said. 'Just you wait and see.'

The first mysterious sound came soon after it became dark. A swish and a swoosh.

James sat bolt upright in his sleeping bag. 'Mandy, did you hear that?'

'Yes,' Mandy replied in a small voice. She was still snuggled down with her sleeping bag pulled right up to her chin. Somehow she felt safer that way.

Blackie was sitting up too, his head cocked on one side, listening.

Suddenly a frantic barking started from below. Pandora and Toby had begun their nightly antics.

'It's really weird.' James shone his torch around the

empty room. 'I don't see how Pandora and Toby could have heard from down there.'

Suddenly Blackie jumped to his feet and began barking too. His bark was so loud that it echoed round and round the little room.

James hurriedly switched on the tape recorder.

When they had managed to calm Blackie down they heard the sounds again. Mrs Ponsonby was right. It *did* sound like someone's long cloak swishing on the ground.

Mandy's heart was beating like a drum. She didn't really believe in ghosts. Or did she? As the noises continued she began to wonder. 'James,' she whispered shakily. 'What do you think it is?'

But James didn't answer. He just sat there, half-in, half-out of his sleeping bag, looking amazed. 'You wait 'til I tell everybody at school about *this*,' he breathed. He shone his torch up to the ceiling. 'It's there,' he hissed. 'Right above us.'

Downstairs, Pandora and Toby were going mad. Mrs Ponsonby had shut them in her bedroom for the night. Blackie was running up and down, barking. Mandy wished he would stop.

James wriggled out of his sleeping bag and shone his torch up to the ceiling. 'Let's have a look in the roof,' he said.

'Do we have to?' Mandy asked.

'Yes.' James was already trying to push open the trapdoor. 'Help me, Mandy,' he panted. 'It's heavy.'

Mandy got out of her sleeping bag to help. She put her shoulder to the trapdoor and heaved. The door suddenly sprang back and hit the rafters with a clang. She stepped back quickly. Something came swooping out and hit the closed window with a thud. Passing, it touched James's hair and face. He gave a little scream of terror and fell backwards. The torch went spinning away. The light went out and plunged them into complete darkness.

Below, Pandora and Toby had stopped making a row. Blackie was quiet too. There seemed to be a dark and dreadful silence.

Mandy switched on her torch. The beam caught something lying on the floor. Something black. She gasped and bent down to get a better look.

It was a bat. Quite a large one, with long, mouse-like ears.

James had found his torch, clicked it on and sat there looking sheepish. 'We should have known it was bats,' he said. 'I was just hoping it was something a bit more exciting.'

'But it *is* exciting,' Mandy breathed. She had forgotten how scared she had been. 'No wonder the dogs could hear things from downstairs. It was the bat's high-frequency squeaks. Dogs can hear much better than humans.'

She carefully picked the creature up. 'Look, it's a mouse-eared bat. I've just been reading about them in my magazine. It's the biggest of all British bats, *and* the rarest. It's thought to be almost extinct. If anyone sees one they've got to write and tell the organisers of something called Bat-watch.'

James peered at the bat and Blackie came over to sniff the little creature. It lay motionless on Mandy's palm. Its huge, waxy wings were spread out on either side of its furry body.

'Wow!' James touched it gently with his fingertip. 'It must have got confused by the torch beam and slammed into the window. Is it dead?'

Mandy shook her head. 'I don't know. I do hope not.'

'We'd better take it to Animal Ark.'

'Yes.'

Suddenly the noise above their heads began again. James hurriedly closed the trapdoor. It sounded as if there was another mouse-eared bat up there. They certainly didn't want that one getting injured too.

They heard a frantic scrabbling sound of paws on the stairs leading up to the attic, then, shortly afterwards, a wary Mrs Ponsonby slowly entered. Toby and Pandora immediately squeezed past her legs and began sniffing round the room, tails waving madly.

'Is everything all right?' Mrs Ponsonby asked dubiously. 'What on earth have you got there?' she said when she saw James was holding something in his hands.

She gave a little scream when they explained. 'Oh, my goodness! A bat! No wonder my darlings were kicking up such a fuss. Horrid thing! You'd better get rid of it.'

'It's not horrid,' Mandy said indignantly. 'It's beautiful . . . and rare. You should be pleased it's chosen to live in your roof.'

Mrs Ponsonby came closer, pulling a face. She gazed at the motionless creature. 'Yes, well, perhaps it isn't *so* horrid . . . Is it dead?'

Mandy explained what had happened. 'We've got to get it to Animal Ark as soon as we can. It could be one of the few of its kind left in the country.'

When Mr Hope answered a midnight knock at Animal Ark's front door, the last thing he expected to see was Mandy and James standing there, Mandy clutching something wrapped in a towel as if it was precious porcelain.

At the kerb, Mrs Ponsonby sat in her sleek saloon car. The electric window slid down and she called, 'I've brought them back . . . they'll explain why.'

'Oh, Mandy!' Mrs Hope came down the stairs, tying the belt of her dressing gown. 'You haven't been a nuisance, have you? I told you—'

'No!' Mandy interrupted. She held out her precious bundle. 'Look.'

She was close to tears as her dad bent to look at the little creature. 'Oh, Dad, please say it won't die.'

Mr Hope's face was grim. 'Bring it into the surgery,' he said. 'I'll see what I can do.'

James had been right. The bat *had* been confused by the torch beam and had lost its bearings. The collision with the window frame had knocked it unconscious.

'No wonder the dogs were going mad,' Mr Hope said with a grin. 'The bats' squeaks would have been driving them crazy.'

But Mandy wasn't in the mood for laughter. 'I don't care about that,' she said. 'I just want him to get well.'

Mr Hope gave her a hug. 'The only thing we can do is keep it warm and keep our fingers crossed that it recovers.'

Mandy visited the bat every few hours. She would lift the lid of its little box and speak softly to the unconscious creature. Mr Hope discovered it was a male. Mandy dubbed him Mickey because of his mouse-like ears.

Then, on the third day, Mickey began to stir. He

opened his little black eyes. Then he opened his mouth and revealed a row of very sharp teeth, just like the one in the article Mandy had read in the wildlife magazine.

Mandy was thrilled. She had been reluctant to contact the magazine in case Mickey didn't survive. Now she felt it safe to do so.

The editor put her in contact with the woman in charge of the bat project. She was overjoyed too.

'A *mouse-eared*!' she said excitedly when Mandy phoned her up. 'That's wonderful!'

'Yes, and we think he's got a mate,' Mandy continued. 'He's fine now, and we're going to take him back this evening.'

'That's terrific. Do you think the owner of the house will let us come and study them when they've settled down again?'

'You'll have to ask her,' Mandy said dubiously.

The woman laughed when Mandy went on to tell her about the ghost.

Mrs Ponsonby quickly recovered from her loss of sleep and was soon back to her normal self: smart clothes, smart hair-do, smart shoes and outrageous hats. She was only too pleased to let the wildlife experts come to study the bats.

She turned up at Animal Ark one day in her smart

car. Pandora and Toby were on velvet cushions in their little compartment at the back.

'I've got some news, dears,' she said, when Mandy answered her impatient knock at the front door.

Oh, no, Mandy thought. *Not more ghosts!*

Mrs Ponsonby told Mandy that a wildlife film company was coming to shoot a film about the bats. 'I always knew Bleakfell Hall would become famous one day,' she said. 'And it's thanks to my darling Pandora and Toby, of course.'

Mandy was so excited at the prospect that she didn't even contradict her.

'What a cheek!' James said later, when she told him what Mrs Ponsonby had said.

Mandy laughed. Then she grew serious. 'I was scared when we were up in that attic though, weren't you?'

James shook his head. Then he nodded and burst out laughing. 'I certainly was. Especially when that bat flew out at me!'

Mandy collapsed with laughter. 'I don't know who was more scared. You, me, or Mrs Ponsonby.'

James chuckled. 'And the really funny thing is that all I've got on the tape is Blackie barking.'

Tears of laughter ran down Mandy's cheeks. 'You can get that any time.'

'I think it's a good idea just to stick to reading books about ghosts in future, don't you?' James snorted.

'Yes,' Mandy said. 'Definitely.'

Blackie gave a loud bark.

'There you are,' James chuckled. 'Blackie thinks it's a good idea too.'

*Look out for more from Mandy and James in the Animal Ark Summer Special, **Ponies at the Point**.*

**If you like ANIMAL ARK –
you'll love JESS THE BORDER COLLIE!
A brand new trilogy from Lucy Daniels!**

Here's an extract from Book 1, *The Arrival* . . .

'Dad!' Jenny yelled across the farmyard.

Fraser Miles turned, and, at the sight of Jenny's worried expression, strode back across the yard towards her. 'What is it?' he asked urgently.

'I don't know,' Jenny replied anxiously. 'Nell seems distressed.'

Fraser followed Jenny into the stables where the sheepdog and her new-born puppies were lying. Nell was panting now, her flanks damp and hot.

Jenny watched as her father put a hand on Nell's side. 'There's another puppy on the way,' he said. 'But I was sure that there were only four. This one must be very small.'

'Is Nell going to be all right?' Jenny asked. 'She wasn't like this with the others. What's wrong, Dad?'

Fraser Miles's face was serious. 'She must be exhausted by now,' he explained.

Jenny closed her eyes and made a wish. *Please let*

them both be all right. She didn't dare to watch. Nell looked up at her with mournful eyes as she struggled to give birth to this last puppy.

'There, girl,' Jenny whispered. 'Just a little longer. Be brave.'

The collie turned her head and licked Jenny's hand. Her body shuddered, then went still. Jenny felt the breath stop in her throat.

'It's OK now,' Fraser reassured her, scooping up a little bundle into his hands. 'It's over, old girl. Just you concentrate on your other four puppies.'

Her father's words rang in Jenny's ears.

'What do you mean, Dad? The last puppy isn't dead, is it?'

Fraser looked down at her and his usually stern expression softened. 'No,' he said gently. 'He isn't dead. But he might as well be. He'll never make a working dog.'

Jenny looked at the pathetic little bundle her father was holding. It was so tiny Fraser could easily hold it in one hand. He had torn away the birth sac from the puppy's head but there was no sign of the little animal breathing. Jenny touched a finger to the puppy's body. It was warm and she could feel his heart beating under his skin.

Then, as her father removed the rest of the sac, the puppy breathed. 'It's going to live!' she cried.

'Look, Jenny,' her father said.

For the first time, Jenny noticed what her father had already seen. The puppy's right front leg was twisted at an impossible angle. 'His leg!' she cried. 'What happened to it?'

'It must have been growing like that for some time inside the womb,' Fraser Miles explained, cutting the umbilical cord and drying the puppy with a piece of old towel.

'Oh, the poor thing,' said Jenny, gently taking the puppy in her own hands. She laid him down beside his brothers and sisters. 'There,' she encouraged him. 'You feed too.'

But the puppy was far too weak. The bigger pups scrambled over him, pushing him out of the way. Even Nell pushed him away from her.

'What's wrong?' Jenny asked. 'Why is Nell rejecting him?'

'Instinct,' her father explained. 'She knows he won't survive. Look at him. He's so weak he can hardly breathe.'

'But he *is* breathing,' Jenny insisted. 'That must mean he wants to live.'

Fraser leaned over and laid his hand on the puppy's bad leg, testing it gently. 'I'd never be able to sell him,' he said.

'I'd look after him,' Jenny protested.

'You know the rules, Jenny,' Fraser Miles answered. 'Every animal on this farm has to earn its keep. This crippled little pup could never do that.'

Jenny blinked back tears. 'What are you going to do then?' she whispered.

Fraser looked at her in real concern. 'I'll have to put him down,' he said gently. 'It's the kindest thing for him. The other puppies will crowd him out. He won't get fed. He won't even get near his mother to keep warm. At least this way he won't be in pain. He won't suffer.'

Jenny swallowed hard. She knew what her father said was true. She had lived on a farm all her life. There was no room for unproductive animals on a farm.

The little puppy moved in her hands and yawned. The tip of a tiny pink tongue licked her finger. Jenny just couldn't let him go – not just yet.

'Can I have a little while to say goodbye?' she asked.

Fraser Miles bent over Nell. 'All right,' he said. 'I'll just wait with Nell to see she's OK after that last birth.'

'Thanks, Dad,' said Jenny. 'I'll take him into the house. It's warmer there and Nell doesn't want him here.'

She was almost at the door when her father called

her. 'Remember what I said, Jenny. Don't get too attached. That puppy has to go.'

Jenny nodded and looked down at the puppy. She knew what her father said made sense. But it was too late. It was *far* too late for common sense. She had already fallen in love with this puppy.

If you'd like to read more – look out for *Jess the Border collie* in the shops from June!

ANIMAL ARK

Lucy Daniels

ANIMAL ACTION

If you like *Animal Ark* then you'll love the RSPCA's Animal Action Club! Anyone aged 13 or under can become a member for just £5.50 a year. Join up and you can look forward to six issues of Animal Action magazine - each one is bursting with animal news, competitions, features, posters and celebrity interviews. Plus we'll send you a fantastic joining pack too!

To be really animal-friendly just complete the form – a photocopy is fine – and send it, with a cheque or postal order for £5.50  (made payable to the RSPCA), to Animal Action Club, RSPCA, Causeway, Horsham, West Sussex RH12 1HG. We'll then send you a joining pack and your first copy of *Animal Action*.

Registered charity no 219099

Don't delay, join today!

Name ....

Address ....

....

....

.... **Postcode** ....

Date of birth ....

Youth membership of the Royal Society for the Prevention of Cruelty to Animals

AACHOD2